# CURIOUS MEN

*Being a Collection of*
*Freaks, Frauds, and Fine Fellows.*
*Gathered by an Eminent Victorian.*

BY
FRANK BUCKLAND

EDITED BY
PAUL COLLINS

THE COLLINS LIBRARY
[A DIV. OF McSWEENEY'S BOOKS]

McSWEENEY'S BOOKS

SAN FRANCISCO

www.mcsweeneys.net

Copyright © 2008

The Collins Library is a series of newly edited and
typeset editions of unusual out-of-print books.

Editor: Paul Collins
Assistant Editor: Jennifer Elder

Cover and interior art is reproduced from Thomas Hood's *Comic Annual*
(1830, 1831, 1835, 1836, 1837, 1838) and from *Comic Magazine* (1833)

ISBN: 978-1-934781-20-3

Printed in Canada.

*Curious Men* is selected and abridged from Frank Buckland's writings; all footnotes are by Buckland, except where indicated by my initials. —*P.C.*

# CONTENTS

# FOREWORD

Have you met the man who walks upside down? The guano mummy? The disembodied singing head of Anthropoglossos? You will.

Whenever a mysterious oddity arrived in Victorian London, readers knew there was one man they could rely on being at the scene: Frank Buckland. A barrel-chested surgeon chomping an ever-present cigar, Buckland was one of the most outsized eccentrics of his time—a naturalist who seriously proposed kangaroo and yak ranching in England, and a raconteur whose London home was filled with a freakish array of stuffed animals and grinning skulls, an all-too-alive menagerie of bickering meerkats, otters, and scorpions, and a gang of monkeys who snatched food off visitors' dinner plates.

Not that his guests were too sorry to miss dinner, since Buckland was also famous as a man who'd eat anything—except earwigs. ("Horribly bitter," he explained.) Fried rotten porpoise, he found, tasted "like a broiled lamp wick." His odd palate was only matched by that of his father, an equally eccentric geologist and respected theologian. When the elder Buckland was shown a miraculous cathedral where "martyrs' blood" accumulated on the stones, the old man dipped his finger in the puddle and tasted it. "I can tell you what it is," he announced to the horrified faithful—"It is bat urine."

Like his earthy yet pious father, Frank Buckland was in fact a deeply religious man. We are all, to Buckland, truly wonderful creations, and this is why he counted many celebrated "freaks" among his best friends. The French giant Joseph Brice once obligingly reached up and wrote his signature on Buckland's ceiling; years later, one of Buckland's nieces recalled watching the amiable giant light his cigar from the top of gas streetlamps. Buckland also had a close friendship with the famed Siamese twins Chang and Eng, one that began when he sent them a unique calling card: a two-headed salmon. The twins were delighted, for they understood his implication: you, too, are a part of this wondrous variety of nature. It was a belief he held to the very end. "I am going on a long journey," he mused on his deathbed in 1880, "where I think I shall see a great many curious animals."

Buckland was one of the era's most beloved writers, and his books went into numerous editions from the 1850s through the early 1900s. Ever since then, Buckland has been the best-kept secret of aficionados of Victorian weirdness. Rescued after a century of obscurity, and culled from thousands of pages of Buckland's eyewitness accounts, *Curious Men* brings back to life eighteen tales from one of the most curious men of all. —*P.C.*

# MEASURING THE GIANT

In the Royal College of Surgeons, Lincoln's Inn Fields, is
the skeleton of a giant who in his day excited great wonder
and curiosity. His name was O'Brian, or Byrne, and he was
commonly known by the title of "the Irish giant." This man was
said to have been eight feet high. I have measured his skeleton
carefully, and find it to be ninety-two and three-quarters inches,
as nearly as possible.*

His history, as quoted from the *Annual Register's Chronicle*,
June 1783, vol. xxxv. p. 209, is as follows: "In Cockspur-street,
Charing-cross, died Mr. Charles Byrne, the famous Irish giant,
whose death was said to have been precipitated by excessive
drinking, but more particularly by the late loss of almost all
his property, which he had simply invested in a single Bank of
England note for £700."

I hear he hid his note in the fireplace in summertime, and
somebody lit the fire and burnt the poor giant's hard earnings.

We have at the College a portrait of this O'Brian; in this old
drawing of his soirée are represented a little doctor (my antitype,

---

* Mr. Cliff told me how this skeleton was procured, or rather purloined, but the
story might not please some of my readers.†

† Buckland revealed the story years later. The great eighteenth-century surgeon
and curiosity-seeker John Hunter, hearing that Byrne was ailing, had his assistant
Mr. Howison ghoulishly trail the giant, so as to procure a rare body for science.
Unnerved by this, O'Brian arranged for burial at sea in a lead coffin, so as to plunge
irretrievably into the depths. Howison intercepted the coffin-bearers at an alehouse,
though, where they agreed upon a bribe of £50. The bearers then suddenly raised
this to £100, and finally to a whopping £500 to turn Byrne's body over. Hunter had
to borrow money to pay it, but pay he did. In a fine bit of turnabout, John Hunter
was himself later exhumed by Buckland. —*P.C.*

I suppose) perched high on a chair measuring his chest, a Life Guardsman (of the period) standing on tiptoe under his arm, and a good-looking young lady showing her pretty "tiny silken-sandal'd" foot by the side of the giant's, the comparison being greatly in the favor of the lady's foot, as far as beauty went.

Though authentic accounts of giants in the flesh are not very common, we find instances innumerable on record of the bones and skeletons of giants having been found buried in the earth. Some laborers who were digging gravel in front of St. John's College, Oxford, discovered and trundled off to my father at Christ Church a wheelbarrow full of "giant's bones," which he immediately decided to be the bones of fossil elephants.

Many accounts are given by ancient authors, such as Kircher and others, not "of gigantic bones only, but of vastly gigantic men found buried underground, or in the hollow caverns of mountains." Of these a learned author, writing in 1722, says: "Remains, such I mean as are truly bone (for some are only natural petrifactions and lapides *sui generis*), were bones belonging to some of the largest sort of fishes of the whale kind; and I am persuaded that the large tooth mentioned by Ol. Wormius was nothing else than the tooth of the *Cetus dentatus* or spermaceti whale."‡

All this I fully endorse. It is a curious passage, and one of the first that began to throw light upon the popular legends and

---

‡ The quotation is from Dr. Thomas Molyneux's "An Essay Concerning Giants." (*Philosophical Transactions*, vol. 22, pages 487–508.) The correct year of publication is 1701. —P.C.

stories of former days, when science was yet young and exhibitions of giants' bones were not uncommon. In 1721, for example, the hand of a giant was publicly shown for money; this hand was being, according to the author above quoted, "the bones of the fore fin of a porpess or small whale artificially joyned together." Here, then, is a good hint for an English Barnum; for the bones of the fin of a porpoise or whale, when the skin has been removed, marvellously resemble in appearance and shape those in the human hand.

# STRANGE CARGO

From giants I now proceed to other human exhibitions. It is seldom, very seldom, that we are invited to see modern mummies, though ancient mummies are not very uncommon. In the month of February 1862, I received an invitation to examine a great natural curiosity described as "The Embalmed Nondescript," then being exhibited at 191 Piccadilly; I hastened to ascertain its nature.

Immediately on viewing it, I exclaimed, "Julia Pastrana!" "Yes, sir," said the proprietor of the exhibition; "it is Julia Pastrana." It may be remembered that some time ago (in 1857) a woman was exhibited in Regent Street, who was remarkable for the immense quantity of long black hair that grew on and about her face. An idea was also attempted to be promulgated that she was not altogether human; and the story was that she had been found among the tribe of Dregig Indians who are reported to inhabit various parts of New Mexico, Oregon, Utah, and the Gulf of Mexico.

Her name was Julia Pastrana. It appears that she died in Moscow, in Russia, and it was stated that she was embalmed there by Professor Suckaloff; and the mummy thus prepared was exhibited in 1862.

Having had some experience in human mummies, I was exceedingly surprised at what I saw. The figure was dressed in the ordinary exhibition costume used in life, and placed erect upon the table. The limbs were by no means shrunken or contracted, the arms, chest, &c. retaining their former roundness and well-formed appearance. The face was marvellous; exactly like an exceedingly good portrait in wax, but it was *not* formed of wax. The

closest examination convinced me that it was the true skin, prepared in some wonderful way; the huge deformed lips and squat
nose remained exactly as in life; and the beard and luxuriant
growth of soft black hair on and about the face were in no respect
changed from their former appearance.

There was no unpleasantness, or disagreeable concomitant, about
the figure; and it was almost difficult to imagine that the mummy
was really that of a human being, and not an artificial model.

I well recollect seeing and speaking to this poor Julia Pastrana
when in life. She was about four feet six inches in height; her eyes
were deep black and somewhat prominent, and their lids had long,
thick eyelashes; her features were simply hideous on account of the
profusion of hair growing on her forehead, and her black beard;
but her figure was exceedingly good and graceful, and her tiny
foot and well-turned ankle, *bien chaussée*, perfection itself. She had
a sweet voice, great taste in music and dancing, and could speak
three languages. She was very charitable, and gave largely to local
institutions of her earnings. I believe her true history was that she
was simply a deformed Mexican Indian woman.* As regards the
history of the embalmment, there were some queer stories told.

In my first series of *Curiosities of Natural History*,† I gave an

---

* Her exhibitor, Theodor Lent, died insane after running onto a bridge and throwing
his money into a river. Pastrana's body disappeared soon afterward, eventually
turning up in Norway in 1921. After being thrown out and then recovered from a
dump in 1979, her mummy was rediscovered at the Oslo Forensic Institute in 1990,
where it still resides today. —P.C.

† A collection of essays by Buckland that first appeared in 1857. —P.C.

account of an exhibition of a modern mummy from the Guano Islands; the name of the man who was preserved in the guano was "Christopher Toledo"; since then I have seen, in a penny show in the streets of Edinburgh, another guano mummy, described in the handbill as follows:

> This mummy was brought to Liverpool from Possession Island, western coast of Africa, by Captain Dunlop, in the schooner *Echo*, from Greenock.
>
> The hair, teeth, whiskers, moustaches, hair on the legs, finger-nails, toe-nails, every part is correct as when alive, and is in a perfect state of preservation. Also will be shown the shirt, stockings, and blanket in which he was buried, and the board which marked his grave on the island, with the date of his interment.
>
> It is shown more to prove the preserving qualities of the guano than from any desire for emolument on the part of the proprietor.

I examined this specimen carefully. On the board (which was made of oak) were rudely carved the words, *Peter Creed, 1790.*

The proprietor was exceedingly proud of his mummy. "There is not a scratch upon him," said he; "he is just as perfect in the back as he is in the front. He is as good as a pension to me as long as he sticks together, and what's good for him is good for me. I cleared £21 in eleven nights with him [rather against the scientific sentiments of the handbill, this]. As for Christopher Toledo, I knows him well enough: *he* did well enough at fust, but he's all going to pieces now, he is; he ain't no use as a scientific mummy now; the more's the luck for me as long as my Peter Creed hold together."

A friend of mine, who now commands a large trading steamer, brought back with him, about two years ago, as a speculation, three mummies from Egypt. Immediately on their arrival from London, he asked me to examine them. They were two males and a female, in a remarkably good state of preservation, the hair, nails, skin, &c. being dry and hard like boards, and the features in two of the specimens distinctly visible. My friend described to me the various adventures and escapes he encountered in bringing over his specimens, it being very difficult to obtain mummies of any kind, nowadays, in consequences of the Egyptian government having forbidden them to be taken out of the country. Among other plans he adopted to pass the authorities who came on board, he placed the three mummies in the berth where the sailors usually sleep, and covered them up with rugs, &c., as though they were tired sailors taking a nap; and if I recollect rightly, he told me that a friend who was a partner in the mummy venture lay down with them.

When the officials came round, the partner pretended to wake up out of sleep, and, sitting up, yawned and rubbed his eyes as if half awake. The deceit answered capitally; the officials, thinking that the three mummies were only three tired sailors, did not examine further, and so they were passed.

In due time these mummies arrived at Liverpool, and the question arose how to sell them to the best advantage; so the owner put it all about the town that some wonderful mummies had just arrived, and were on board the ship in the docks. A paragraph even got into the local newspapers to the same effect, and this was just what they wanted; for a showman who had an exhibition in the town, reading the account in the newspaper, immediately came onboard the ship and made a bid for the mummies. The price tendered, however, was not high enough.

The next day the showman came again with a further offer, which, however, was not accepted. To make him more desirous of obtaining the curiosities, my friends found out where his show was situated, and for two or three evenings remained smoking their cigars about the show, and paid boys and idle people they found about the place a small fee to go to the door of the show and ask to "see the wonderful mummies which had just arrived."

"We have not got them yet, sir," was the showman's answer.

"What? Not got the mummies! Never heard such a thing. No mummies! Can't possibly go into the show," said the visitors.

The fact of so many people coming, night after night, so quickened the showman's appetite that he made a higher bid of several hundred pounds, which offer, foolishly, not being accepted, the owners brought the mummies up to London.

The last thing I heard of them was from my friend, who told me that he had left his mummies at his lodgings while he went on another voyage; when he returned, he found his landlord had got into trouble, and had *pawned* the mummies for £10 at some pawnbroker's by the Docks. Reader, if you are very anxious to have them, there may still be a chance of getting the mummies cheap.

# OCCUPATIONS
# FOR CHILDREN

I always go into caravan exhibitions at fairs, &c. At the Windsor Fair, in 1861, I saw, hanging outside a show, a large picture of "The Spotted Child, to be seen alive." I paid my penny, but as the Spotted Child did not come in just at the moment, and I was in a hurry, I paid sixpence for an immediate and private view of the Spotted Child; and the woman who had charge of the show brought out from behind the curtain an exceedingly pretty little flaxen-haired, blue-eyed English girl, dressed in ordinary costume, about six years old. I could see spots about her, but her mother soon showed me that her body, arms, and legs were all covered with spots of different shapes and sizes.

I examined these spots carefully with a pocket magnifying lens, and have no hesitation at all in saying that they were the result of no skin disease at all, which I thought before I saw the child might have been the case, but were simply marks made by a strong solution of nitrate of silver which had stained the skin a jet black, and which showed up well on her white skin. I could perceive, with a magnifying glass, even the marks of the brush at the edges of the spots.

Ladies may like to know that the application of nitrate of silver would not in any way hurt the child, and they would soon wear off.* The mother was an ingenious woman thus to turn her child to account without in any way injuring it.

---

\* Though useful as a topical antibacterial, nitrate of silver is not as harmless as Buckland implies. Those taking silver internally also risk *argyria*, which colors the eyes, mouth, and skin. Its most famous sufferer is Stan Jones, a libertarian candidate for the U.S. Senate in Montana's 2002 elections. During the campaign, Jones's entire body turned permanently blue. He did not win his race. —*P.C.*

# WANDERING
# MOUNTEBANKS

I n the London streets, the spectators are, to me, themselves the greatest show. As Pope has it, translating Homer's allusion to the Roman sports—

Let bear or elephant be e'er so white
The people, sure the people, are the sight.

I never neglect any opportunity of learning how some of the more needy of the mixed multitude endeavor to gain a scanty living, and transfer a few coins from the pockets of their richer fellows to their own.

The Epsom Downs, on Derby Day especially, seem to be the assembling point of all the peripatetic performers for a hundred miles round; real vagabonds some of them, honest kindly folks others; but all anxious to make a harvest. I was gazing one Derby Day on the crowd, from the top of the 2nd Life Guards' drag, when I was startled by a sudden and most hideous noise at my shoulder. Turning round, I beheld a man with an enormous shock of wool-like hair, stuck out from his head like a New Mexican savage, who, holding his nose with his fingers, was producing, with marvelous intonation, the most unmusical bray of a donkey; he must have practiced it for years, for it was louder and more discordant than the real donkey's voice, and the prolonged screech at the end caused many bystanders to put their hands to their ears in sheer despair.

Then a pale-looking man, with his hair cut quite short, and clad in a tight-fitting jersey which seemed quite wet through, deposited by the door of the drag a washing tub nearly half full of water. I could not imagine what he was going to do, till he threw into the tub a small coin, meant as a decoy for other contributions, and, pulling his short hair, said, "American diver, if you please, sir."* By dint of practice, he had acquired skill in fishing up coins with his lips; a performance not interesting to see, and anything but conducive to the longevity of the diver, whose head was sometimes submerged a painfully long time.

Following him came a man with an electric machine, and he gave shocks at the rate of a penny a shock, or three shocks for twopence; he did not get many customers at the latter tariff, but one pocket of his old tall-coat seemed pretty heavy with subscriptions to this scientific experimental philosopher.†

"The fire-eater, or the celebrated living salamander," growled out a deep voice close under the wheel of the drag, while I was speaking to a friend. "Light up, Jim," said the wild-looking owner of the voice aforesaid. Jim forthwith put a penny tinplate on the ground, and, pulling some dirty tow out of one pocket and some

---

* His job title had a truly fearless originator. Now forgotten, the twenty-three-year-old American seaman Michael Smith astounded Britain with a daring leap high off the Sunderland Bridge and into the River Wear in 1842. Reports the *Illustrated London News* for September 17th: "Smith has done what no man ever did before; and, very probably, what no other man will ever dare attempt again... He has frequently leaped from the highest yards and masts into the sea." Pulling himself out of the River Wear to the hearty cheers of the assembled crowd, Smith was then duly arrested for trespassing. —*P.C.*

† This was apparently a splendid enough diversion that in 1923 one Valentine Johnson published *Electrical Recreations*, a guide to such hazardous party tricks as shocking dear friends with electrified wine glasses, electrified picture frames, electrified cats, etc. —*P.C.*

powdered resin out of the other, placed them both on the plate, and lighted them up according to orders. The living salamander coolly began cutting up his smoking and indigestible meal with a knife and a fork, and, when sufficiently comminuted, ate it all up, bit by bit, hot, blazing, and emitting fumes of resin! Why he did not burn his lips and mouth, I know not, and where he stowed it all away, I am amazed to understand; certain it is, he brought none of it out again in my presence; he must have a pouch like a pelican somewhere in his throat, for immediately after his fiery meal he devoured a hatful of shreds of paper, and then, making sundry grimaces, pulled out of his mouth a long roll of particolored paper, a yard and a half long, coiled up in a beautiful tapering cone.

What an apparition! Surely it is a ghost making its way toward me among the wheels of the carriages. Not a word nor a sound does it utter, and how carefully it glides along. Poor ghost, you must indeed be hungry to allow your body to be converted into a walking advertisement! The ambitious card engraver who hired you deserves some credit for the pattern of your coat; cunning man was he who thought of clothing you in a long, sleeveless garment, and sewing the business and visiting cards of his customers onto it, so that you look like a mountain of white, green, and other diverse-colored cards. Your head may have but little brains inside; but anyhow, the outside affords a fixed point whereon to fasten a huge cardboard cocked hat, with a card weathercock upon it bearing the name of your employer the card engraver (whose name, notwithstanding all the trouble he has taken to impress it upon me, I forget). Poor ghost, we hope you are well-paid for your labor!

I then witnessed a very curious exhibition, viz. the "stone-cracker." A man comes in front of the drag and fixes a small square board, supported on a pole, into the ground. He then produces from a sack a stone. He places the stone on the board, flourishes his arm about in the air, and then bringing his closed fist suddenly down upon the stone, cracks it as though his hand were an iron hammer. I got the stone-cracker to turn stones out of the sack for me to examine. They were ordinary stones, picked up from the roadside, generally about the size of a man's double-fist, and consisted of lumps of flint, limestone, and even granite. I plucked out a bit of grey Guernsey granite (evidently a portion of our London street-paving stone), and placed it on the board to be cracked. The stone-cracker gave it a sharp blow with his fist, and it fell in halves in a moment. I examined the man's hand. The portion of his hand which acted as the head of the hammer was the pad of flesh by the little finger which forms the outside of the hand. The skin &c. here was formed, from frequent stone-breakings, into a solid hornlike mass, but his arm and forearm did not seem to be particularly well developed, not so well as we see in regimental farriers and blacksmiths.

I conclude, therefore, that the stones are cracked more by a peculiar knack of hitting them than by actual force. I have the bit of granite I saw broken by the stone-cracker in my museum; it is nearly two inches thick. This curious performer boasted that he could crack a millstone with his fist, and I believe it is possible if the stone was of colite, and not over-thick in substance.

Since the first edition of this book was published, I have received the following:

155 Southgate Road, N. 13th February, 1866

Dear Sir — In your interesting work, you introduce the stone-cracker to your readers, and make the following remark: 'I conclude, therefore, that the stones are cracked more by a peculiar knack of hitting than by actual force.' If at all interesting to you, I beg to offer the following as an explanation of how the trick is done. About half a dozen years ago I was at Dover Regatta, and there saw a lame man break stones in the following manner. He first placed a small wooden stool upon the ground, and then produced a piece of rag, which (having first unfolded to show that nothing was concealed within it) he wound round his right hand, crossing it over the palm and back, and excluding the thumb. He said that he wore this to prevent splinters from cutting his flesh. Having done this, he pulled from a bag a stone and a piece of granite, each about the size of a man's hand, and from two to three inches thick; he then placed the granite firmly upon the stool, and the flint he held with his left hand, apparently resting it upon the top of the granite. Then giving his right arm one or two swings in the air, and uttering a shout, he (with the covered portion of his hand) hit the flint, and split it in two. Being considerably astonished at this apparently extraordinary feat, I waited, and saw it repeated; and then I noticed that during the time he was swinging his arm, he quietly raised the flint stone about half an inch from the granite, so that, when he gave the blow, the former received a sharp concussion from coming in contact with the granite, and this, I presume, caused the fracture.

By keeping the above plain in view, I was able to crack, with comparative ease, the same kind of stone as the performer did, and found that very little practice was required.

Yours obediently,

B.F. DAVIES.

# CATCH-PENNIES

The edges of certain pavements in London have become regular markets for semigratuitous exhibitions.

There used formerly to be a man, who stood in Leicester Square, who sold microscopes at a penny each. They were made out of a common pillbox; the bottom being taken out, and a piece of window glass substituted. A small eyehole was bored in the lid, and thereon was placed the lens, the whole apparatus being painted black. Upon looking through one of these microscopes, I saw hundreds of creatures, which I at once recognized as paste eels, swimming about in all directions; yet on the object-glass nothing could be seen but a small speck of flour and water, conveyed there on the end of a lucifer match from a common inkstand, which was nearly full of this vivified paste. Another microscope exhibited a single representative of the animal kingdom, a parasite of our own race, showing his impatience of imprisonment by kicking vigorously. I could not help admiring the beauties of construction in this little monster, which, if at liberty, would have excited murderous feelings, unfavorable to the promulgation of his existence. The sharp-pointed mouth, with which he works his diggings; his side-claws, wherewith to hold on while at work; the little heart, pulsating slowly but forcibly, sending a stream of blood down the large vessel in the center of his white and transparent body—all could be seen and wondered at. When the stock of this sort of live game runs short, a common carrot seed is substituted; which, when looked at through a magnifier, is marvelously like an animal, having a thick body and numerous legs projecting from the sides; so like an animal that it has been mistaken by an enthusiastic philosopher for one created in, or by, a chemical mixture in conjunction with electricity; at least, my father always declared that the insects created by the late Mr. Crosse were simply carrot seeds.

I bought several of these microscopes, and determined to find out how all this could be done for a penny. I took them to my friend, the late Professor Queckett,* and we examined them together. We found that their magnifying power was of about twenty diameters. The cost of a lens made of glass, of such a power, would be three or four shillings. How, then, could the whole apparatus be made for a single penny? A penknife revealed the mystery. The pillbox was cut in two, and then it appeared that the lens was made of Canada balsam. The balsam had been heated, and, when it had assumed the proper size, shape, transparency, and polish of a well-ground glass lens, it had been carefully dropped onto the eyehole of the pillbox. Our ingenious lens-maker informed me that he had been selling these microscopes for fifteen years, and that he and his family conjointly made them. One child cut out the pillboxes, another put them together, his wife painted them black, and he made the lenses.

Not long afterward, in another part of the town, I came

---

\* John Thomas Quekett (1815–1861), president of the Royal Society of Surgeons and a great popularizer of the microscope. Upon turning his attention to adulterants in food, Quekett shocked Londoners by discovering calves' brains and other offal in milk. —P.C.

across another microscopist. He did not sell anything, but merely charged a halfpenny for a peep. His apparatus consisted of a tin box, the size of a common tea caddy, placed on three legs, at about the level of a small boy's eye: these ingenious youths being his principal customers. The fee being paid, the slide was drawn away from the peephole, and the observer addressed in the following words: "Here you see a drop of Thames water, which looks like a gallon; the water is full of heels, snakes, and hadders a-playing about and a-devouring of one another." It was filled with numerous little creatures, which, having very small bodies, have as a sort of compensation received very large Latin names from their discoverer. Many of them were swimming about, pursued by what appeared to be immense sea snakes. Others were quietly reposing on weeds, which looked like elm trees, and all of them were perfectly unconscious of being exhibited to the British public at a halfpenny a head. But this was not all: the exhibitor next brought out of his waistcoat pocket a small tin tube, and said, all in one breath, "There you see a flea chained round his neck with a silver chain he lays his heggs on the glass and I feeds him three times a day on my 'and—the performance is now concluded."

In Tothill Street, Westminster, or the Tottenham Court Road, on a Saturday night, when what I call the "Poor Man's Market" is going on, a glassblower may sometimes be seen, who goes his rounds to sell the products of his industry. A glass pen, a glass Napoleon's trident, a glass dove fastened to the top of a pointed wire so as to form a breast pin, and a glass peacock with a beautiful tail of spun glass are wrapped in a neatly made brown paper bag, and sold for the sum of one penny.

Workers in iron also endeavor to catch an honest penny. There is a man who sells for twopence a most ingenious contrivance for roasting meat. It consists of no less than five pieces of iron wire, which, when put together, are strong enough to hold up a good-sized leg of mutton. One of the pieces serves as a fastening to the mantelpiece, and the others are attached to it by one of the pieces aforesaid. The cook is enabled by a simple mechanism, not unworthy of a Brunel or Stephenson, to heighten or lower the meat according to the state of the fire. If the inventor of this apparatus had a chance, there is no telling how many benefits he might confer upon mankind, and, let us hope, upon himself too, by his mechanical talents.

In Leicester Square, where penny-catchers congregate most, razor paste, at one penny a box, is sold by a dexterous shaver, who chops such large gashes in a bit of wood with a shilling razor that he makes the wood fly about. He then passes the blunted instrument a few times over his magic strop, and, pulling a hair from his head, divides it as it stands erect between his finger and thumb, with the same ease with which Saladin divided the scarf with his scimitar, and the Life Guardsmen, at an assault of arms, cuts a sheep in half with his broadsword. The paste is, very likely (and so is the razor), more efficacious in the hands of the proprietor than of the purchaser; nevertheless, it is a good pennyworth.

I am forming a collection of various articles bought for one penny in London streets;† and I would beg my reader not to pass by these ingenious, poor, hardworking people. Those who do not condescend to go into the "Poor Man's Market," especially on a Saturday night in the streets of London, can have no idea what ingenuity and perseverance is shown to procure a subsistence. Thus, outside the Cattle Show, was a noble-looking old fellow who was selling "The Queen for a penny." I bought a pocketful of statues representing Her Most Gracious Majesty. The Queen is made of thin wax, but really the statue is not bad at all. The old man also had statues of Napoleon, the Sultan, the Emperor of Germany, &c., all at one penny. Who would not buy a potentate at the price?

---

† Curiously, this was not a new idea. In 1677 Henry Peacham published *The Worth of a Penny; or, a Caution to Keep Money, with the Causes of Scarcity and Misery of Want Thereof, in these Hard and Merciless Times, &c.* Among the penny bargains Peacham lists are a dish of coffee, or "news in England, and in other Countries, of Murders, Floods, Witches, Fires, Tempests, and whatnot, in the Weekly news-books." Or: "you may have your dog wormed, and so be kept from running mad." But a penny only went so far, even in 1677—"For a penny you may buy a fair cucumber; but not a breast of Mutton, except it be multiplied." —*P.C.*

# BARNUM'S NEXT EXHIBIT

A SAWRIAN.

Fond as the English people are of comparing notes as to mutual progress, whether in Nature or Art, by means of public exhibition, they have not yet arrived at the idea of exhibiting samples of themselves. Our American cousins, on the contrary, exhibit living specimens of the rising generation.

Barnum, the king of showmen, having exhibited almost everything in creation, has actually and positively duly advertised and invited the inhabitants of Boston to visit his Baby Show.*

Of this I have certain and good evidence; for Mrs. Blackwell—the wife of my cousin, the late Thos. Blackwell, Esquire, Engineer to the Grand Trunk Railway, Canada—lately returned from her travels in America, has kindly put into my hands the bill of this Baby Show:

---

* Barnum's first Baby Show, held in Manhattan in June 1855, attracted sixty thousand visitors and much controversy. Imitators followed, including those specializing in "Colored Baby Shows." Barnum himself returned to the format in various cities in 1862. Visiting the first June 1855 show, the *New York Times* reported: "The bad jokes and outrageous puns were worse than the heat. The latter made one lady faint away—the former spoiled hundreds of appetites for dinner." —*P.C.*

# Barnum's Museum,

Every Day and Evening this Week,

commencing Monday,

June 2nd, 1862.

### GRAND NATIONAL

# BABY SHOW!!!

## 100 BEAUTIFUL BABIES

Will be on exhibition for prizes, for which upward of

2,000 DOLLARS CASH WILL BE DISTRIBUTED FOR THE

FINEST BABIES, TWINS, TRIPLETS, QUATERNS, AND

## FAT BABIES!

Amongst the babies is one from Cincinnati, Ohio,

### 8 MONTHS OLD, WEIGHING BUT

### 1 POUND 7 OUNCES.

The smallest speck of living humanity ever seen.

An ordinary ring finger slips easily over its hand

and arm to the elbow. No conception can be formed

of the exceeding diminutiveness of this little atom

of the human race, which is really the

## GREATEST WONDER OF THE WORLD!

There are also

# THIRTY-TWO PAIRS OF TWINS,
# FOUR TRIPLETS,

And numerous FAT BABIES, besides the great number of single Babies, making it the

# GREATEST GALAXY
# OF HUMAN WONDERS
# EVER BEHELD!!!

The Premiums will be distributed among the most meritorious by Lady Judges of the highest respectability.

The Premiums range from 500 dols.! 250 dols.! 150 dols.! 100 dols.! 50 dols.! down to 5 dols.! and in all *over seventy cash premiums will be awarded!*

The Babies will be on exhibition every day from 11 a.m. till 3 p.m., and from 7 till 8 p.m., in the following order:

MONDAY, JUNE 2nd—From 11 a.m. till 3 p.m., Babies of all ages will be exhibited.

First premium declared at 3 p.m. From 7 p.m. till 8 p.m. This and each other evening, Babies, Twins, Triplets, Quaterns, and Fat Babies over 4 years of age.

TUESDAY, JUNE 3rd—From 11 a.m. till 3 p.m., Babies under 1 year of age exhibited.

WEDNESDAY JUNE 4th—From 11 a.m. till 3 p.m.,
Babies from 1 to 3 years of age, and Babies from 3 to 5 years
exhibited in two different classes.
Premiums declared at 3 p.m.

THURSDAY, JUNE 5th—From 11 a.m. till 3 p.m.,
all the Premium Children exhibited.

FRIDAY, JUNE 6th—From 11 a.m. till 3 p.m.,
all the Premium Children exhibited.

SATURDAY, JUNE 7th—From 11 a.m. till 3 p.m.,
all the Premium Children exhibited.

All the Twins, Triplets, Quaterns, and Fat Children,
as well as the Baby taking the highest premiums, to be seen
on the 2nd, 3rd, 4th, 5th, 6th, and 7th of June,
from 11 a.m. till 3 p.m.

Ladies and Children desirous of avoiding the discomforts of
a great crowd will do well to come early in the morning,
and see the Museum and other Curiosities before the Baby
Show commences. Not later than 9 or 10 o'clock.

Walker and Sneden's Self-rocking Cradles, highly recommended by Physicians, and also Dr. Brown's celebrated
patented Baby Tender, have been provided for
the use and comfort of the Babies.

My informant tells me that, according to the wish expressed in the bill, she attended early, but even then found the room crowded with visitors. The babies were arranged in two rows along the side of the room. The very tiny ones were held in their nurses' arms, who sat on chairs on the level of the floor; separated, however, from too-anxious admirers by a strong handrail.

Above and at the back of the row of nurses was erected a platform, and upon the platform were exhibited the elder babies, each one in a separate chair, into which it was judiciously and carefully fastened, so that falling out was impossible.

Strange to say, these babies were very good and quiet; they did not tumble or twist about, or cry, or behave themselves in any way that did not become a baby exhibited in public. The fat babies were especially quiet, for they went fast asleep in spite of the crowds of people looking at them.

The "Cincinnati speck of humanity" was not well enough to be always on view; so, at stated periods, a bell rang, and it was brought out for examination. This poor little creature excited great curiosity among the visitors. I wondered much that the poor babies did not cry; but I understand that American babies are not like European babies—they express no sentiments whatever till after they are three years old.

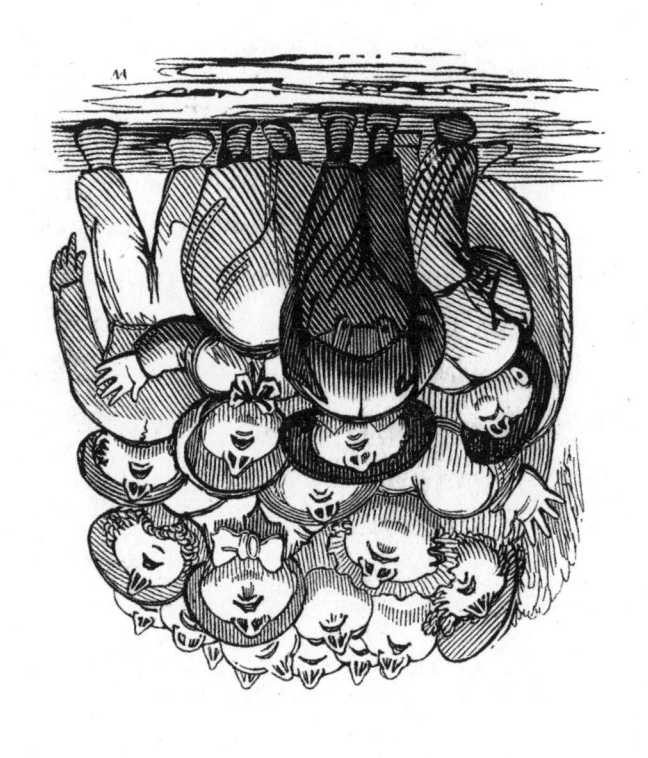

THE CEILING WALKER

In November 1862, the London streets were placarded with the single word *Olmar*. This mysterious announcement proved to signify that a performer bearing that naming was about to become a candidate for public patronage. No clue being given in the advertisement to the nature of his performances, I, of course, was anxious to see in what they consisted; and now I venture to give some idea of the really terrific performance of Olmar.

The visitor, on entering the Alhambra in Leicester Square, noticed suspended far above his head a ladder, a trapeze swing, and a square-shaped wooden frame, from the sides of which depended large rings. It almost made one giddy to look up from below at the gymnastic arrangement, which was about ninety feet above one's head; and one shuddered to think that a human being could possibly display feats of activity at such a height in the air.

However, at the appointed time, Olmar appeared; and, after a series of feats on the trapeze and the ladder suspended in mid-air at this frightful height—feats which made one's blood run cold to look at—he began to walk with his head downward. He ascended, this time, to the square frame of the building as before stated, at a height of about ninety feet from the floor of the building. On to the lower side of the frame were affixed rings (about large enough to admit a Dutch cheese), of which there were nine on each side of the square. He surveyed them for a moment, and then, quickly reversing himself on the rope, placed a foot in one of the rings, hanging *head downward*. He then let go of his supporting rope, placed the free foot in the next ring, and so walked away with his feet in the ring—his head being downward—right round the sides of the square. He went along at a very good pace, and I observed he managed to twist his head up every now and then, to see that he did not miss the ring with his foot. This performance was really fearful to behold.

After ascending again to a ladder, he took a terrific jump from one side of it, and, passing through the air the whole length of the ladder, caught hold of the other end on the outside; in fact, he jumped the length of the ladder by passing *along its side* in the air—exactly the leap of one of the spider monkeys at the Zoological—only that Olmar being a man had not prehensile feet nor a prehensile tail to assist him. He then twined *one* leg in the rope, which was now again brought within his reach, and descended slowly and gracefully, with a twisting motion, to the earth again; and right glad I should imagine he was to get there once more safely.

These performances are most fraught with danger, imminent, literally, at every step. To go through them must require pluck more than human beings generally possess—nerves and limbs of iron, quickness of motion and thought, combined with steadiness and agility. Accordingly, we see all these characteristics well marked in the personal features of Olmar.

The performance concluded, I had a lengthened interview with Olmar, who kindly allowed me to make an examination of his physique. He is not a tall man, but is all muscle and strength: the power of his biceps and forearm is tremendous; his wrist has amazing strength in it; his pectoral muscles project like the breast of a bird; the muscles in his back are like those in the figures of Hercules in the statues by Roubiliac in Westminster Abbey; his chest has a large capacity; and he weighs, with all this power, but 130 lbs. It was very curious, also, to observe how certain muscles in the abdomen and back, not developed in ordinary persons, are very much developed in Olmar. They are the very muscles which are called into play when he walks on the rings head downward, and plainly show us how nature has provided muscles for the working of the human frame in whatever position it may be placed—even when the head is downward.

Olmar told me that his ladder was made of the best Jamaican lancewood; the bar of the trapeze was four-and-a-half feet long and two inches in diameter; the apparatus with the rings (which are iron covered in rope) was ninety feet from the floor of the Alhambra.

He was eleven years learning to walk in the rings head downward,* and it was nine years before he had confidence enough in himself to perform in public. The great difficulty he experienced at first was to "keep the blood out of his head" when in this position, and it was ten months before he trained his head to it.

It was no trick, but simply a feat requiring great courage and coolness. When near the ground, he could walk along 150 to 170 rings without difficulty. He showed me the amazing power of his foot; for when he bent his toes upward, it was only with difficulty that I could force the foot down again. The tendons working the feet are as strong as iron wires.

---

* This routine, notes Ricky Jay in his *Journal of Anomalies*, appears to have been first performed by a Mr. Sanches in 1806. Later variants of ceiling walking also used powerful vacuum-suction shoes and electromagnetic boots. —*P.C.*

He learned his aerial walking lesson gradually, as a little child learns to walk on the floor of the nursery; even then, he was obliged to practice by himself every morning. He considered his most difficult feat to be balancing himself by one foot on the trapeze bar, even when the bar was close to the ground. He knew no other professional who could do it; the bar is so apt to slip away from under the foot, for it is very unsteady, and trembled greatly under his weight.

Olmar, I was pleased to see, was not inclined to "swagger" or be conceited about his performance: he acknowledged its danger, but long practice, perseverance, coolness, pluck, and strength enabled him to overcome this danger. He had never yet met with an accident;[†] and trusted that his personal qualities, with great care in fixing the apparatus, would enable him to escape harm or injury for the future.

---

† Olmar—the stage of name of James Chadwick—did indeed later fall from the ceiling of the Alhambra. Chadwick's resulting broken thigh ended his upside-down career. —P.C.

# THE HUMAN FROG

On Saturday, August 10, 1867, I was invited by Mr. E.R. Adams, the polite and active secretary of Cremorne Gardens, to give some account, in *Land and Water*, of a most curious subaqueous performance. A huge human aquarium (for I can call it nothing else) is placed on the stage. It is made of iron, with a plate-glass front, and measures nine feet by five. It contains four tons of water, the depth being about six feet. It cost nearly £100. When I arrived, the "human frog" had just begun his performance, and through the plate-glass I beheld a human form twisting itself round and round with the velocity of a cockchafer on a pin, and looking like a huge jack fighting in his last efforts to get rid of the fatal gorge-bait.

The following is a list of the "Natator"'s subaqueous performances. Firstly, he stands on his head; his head touches the bottom of the aquarium, and his feet are at the top, like a couple of huge fishing floats. This is called the "minute trick," and is performed first in order to show the longest time that "Natator" can stay under water.

His second performance is to swim up and down the tank several times—twenty at the most—without coming once to the surface to breathe. He twists himself right round, and gives a slight push with his foot at each end of the tank, so as to reverse his motion. This is a very difficult trick, inasmuch as the aquarium is not long enough for him to make a clean stroke, and he has to stop his force at either end as well as he can. The performance requires from forty to forty-five seconds under water.

Thirdly, "Natator" sits down (tailor fashion) at the bottom

of the aquarium, and grins at the people through the plate-glass front. He opens and shuts his eyes under water, to show that this can be done. He also opens his mouth quite wide under the water; this, he tells me, is very difficult. Great practice has enabled him to do it without swallowing a drop of water. He throws out air bubbles once, and once only; this is necessary to enable him to sink to the bottom. While there, he neither emits air bubbles nor, being under water (of course), takes in a fresh supply of air.

Fourthly, he again descends, and eats, under water, a sponge cake or a bun. He opens his mouth to show that he has really swallowed it. It is most difficult to swallow cake under water without also swallowing water. It required three years' practice to do this performance with safety; for if, when under water, he should happen to cough, the water would enter, he would instantly be choked, and a serious accident would ensue.

Fifthly, ascending to the surface, a soda-water bottle is handed to him; he dives with it to his perch at the bottom and drinks down the contents, viz. a halfpenny worth of milk; he chooses milk because of the color, and in order that the audience may see that he actually drinks it from the bottle; this is a most difficult trick, as it is hard to swallow the milk without water getting into the mouth.

Sixthly, a lighted pipe is handed to him; he takes a few whiffs of it above the water, and then descends with it; when under water, he manages somehow to keep it alight, and to emit bubbles, which, rising through the water, burst in little puffs of tobacco smoke. Coming to the surface, he shows that his pipe is still alight.

Seventhly, he does "poses plastiques" under water, placing

himself in various attitudes, and then the piano strikes up the tune of "Froggy would a-wooing go." The "human frog" dances to the music, frog fashion, at the bottom of the water, all the while singing the song. It is very curious to see the bubbles of air from his mouth, rushing up to the surface in greater or less profusion according to the number of words in the verse of a song which the spectator should follow in his mind. This would be an interesting study for Professor Wheatstone or Tyndall, to see how many bubbles of air were necessary to form an individual word. "Natator" tells me he can hear the piano quite plainly, when under the water; this was indeed evident from the way his bubbles kept time with the music; and he also tells me that if anyone speaks very loud outside the glass, he can hear him plainly. This bears on the question of fish hearing under water; but it must be recollected that a fish's ear is very differently constructed than a human one. We humans have no otoliths—a peculiar bony structure found in the fish's ear only. This otolith structure is necessary for hearing under water, for we find that the whale, in other respects an air-breathing, warm-blooded animal, with a four-cavitied heart, has his ear fashioned after the pattern of that of a fish.

Eighthly, "Natator" swims with a jerking motion like a shrimp, with a steady but sudden rush like a jack, with a lazy, sleepy floating like a hundred-year-old carp in the royal ponds in Virginia Water; and lastly, being apparently seized with a fit of the "merry-go-rounds," performs a series of head-over-heels gyrations round and round, like a man practicing upon a pole between bars in a school of gymnastics. He remains in midwater, without touching the top or bottom of the tank, the whole time, and does not once come to the surface; this might well be called the "porpoise trick." The greatest number of head-over-heels turns that he performs (and this generally every night) is twenty-four, and he requires about fifty seconds to get through them.

The performance concluded, "Natator" allowed me to examine him in my medical capacity. He is a young man, twenty years old, five feet seven-and-a-half inches in stature, and nine stone six lbs. in weight; he is lightly built, but exceedingly well made and muscular. With all his hard and very peculiar work, "Natator" (whose name, he has no objection to my stating, is Cooper,[*] well known to professional swimmers) has excellent health. When he first began to practice long stays under water, some four years since, he used to suffer from severe headaches, but now these have quite disappeared; he never has rheumatism, or other aches or pains in any form, though he goes through his performance at half past ten every night, and sometimes twice a day. The water in his aquarium he generally manages to keep at a temperature of about 62 degrees, but the warmer the water is, the longer he can stay in, and the easier his performances become. He nearly had a bad accident with the first aquarium that was made for him;[†]

---

[*] Later performers in the 1870s and 1880s appear to have lifted Cooper's act and name, including Professor Charles "Man-Fish" Beach and Thomas Weightman; the latter toured New Zealand claiming to be Buckland's "Natator." —P.C.

[†] Terrariums and then aquariums were invented around 1829 by Whitechapel surgeon and botanist Nathaniel Bagshaw Ward. His plate-glass cases launched a Victorian craze for household ferns and fishkeeping, and in succeeding decades large-scale water spectacles also became popular with the public. —P.C.

the front was composed of one large piece of plate-glass. Just as he was about, at rehearsal, to get into the water, the glass gave way with a sudden crash, and washed him with terrible force into the orchestra, which was instantly flooded. If he had been inside the aquarium, and not providentially outside, he might have been killed by the rush of water through the fractured glass. This glass is now subdivided into four, with a strong iron frame, and the aquarium is perfectly safe.

# TWO HEADS...

I must now describe the "Two-Headed Nightingale." The Siamese Twins were certainly very wonderful people, but in Millie-Christine we have, I think, something more remarkable. The Siamese Twins are two old gentlemen somewhat advanced in years. The "Two-Headed Nightingale" is composed of two charming young negress girls, who are united back to back by an indissoluble bond. I do not recollect having seen a more intelligent, ever-laughing happy face than that of Miss Christine. She has dark rolling eyes and jet-black hair, and a quickness and intelligence about her that shows her culture and education.

Millie is like her sister in face and in her charming manners. They live in perfect concord, and from long habit walk about and even dance without any appearance of effort or constraint. They are called the "Two-Headed Nightingale" because they both sing very well, and the duets they practice show they have good voices, which have been successfully cultivated. Their age is nineteen.*

Dr. Bowerbank, of St. Leonards, was kind enough to send me a specimen of the common English snake (*Coluber natrix*), that was blessed with two heads. This "double-headed nightingale" among snakes is six inches long, and evidently had not long survived his,

---

* Millie-Christine McKoy had been in London before, having been kidnapped out of slavery by an exhibitor; a detective captured and returned the children to their North Carolina plantation. After Emancipation, they toured into the early twentieth century as famed and business-savvy vaudeville performers, able to demand up to $25,000 for a show. They were talented at the piano and singing— rather conveniently, Millie was a contralto, and Christine was a soprano. —P.C.

her, or their birth. The left head is a little larger than the right head, which grows, as it were, out of the side of the beast. The left head has a fair-sized neck; the right head, so to speak, has no neck at all. The left head, therefore, may be considered to be the head proper, the right the secondary head.

Double-headedness is not uncommon among snakes and fishes. There are in the College of Surgeons two specimens of double-headed snakes. One is, as in this instance, the common English yellow-ringed snake; the other is a small American snake. Every year I have one or two double-headed salmon hatched out in my breeding boxes. They generally live about three weeks, and then die simultaneously. The gills in these double-headed salmon both breathe, but I have never seen them feed.

I once read an account of a double-headed catfish (*Anarhichas lupus*) having been caught in the North Sea. What a valuable specimen this would be. In the College of Surgeons, there is a specimen of a foetal dogfish (*Squalus canicula*) with two perfect heads, which unite in one body behind the gills. Double-headedness is also frequently found in calves, lambs, kittens, and chickens.

The most remarkable specimen that I know of is a preparation, in the Royal College of Surgeons, of the double skull of a double-headed male child, born in May 1783, in the province of Burdwan, in Bengal. These skulls are placed one on top of the other, and united in this position. Even though the two heads were united, the child lived to be four years old, and, strange to say, died from the poison bite of a cobra.

# FLEAS TO MEET YOU

In the month of July 1856, I discovered an individual who for twenty years had devoted his life to the intellectual training of fleas. He carried on his operations in a little room in Marylebone Street, London. I entered, and saw fleas here, fleas there, fleas everywhere; no less than sixty fleas imprisoned and sentenced to hard labor for life. All of them were luckily chained, or fastened in some way or other, so that escape and subsequent feasting upon visitors was impossible. A little black speck jumps up suddenly off the table whereon the performance takes place— I walk up to inspect, and find that it is a monster flea attired "à la convict": he is free to move about, but, wherever he goes, a long gilt chain, tightly fastened round his neck, accompanies him.

Occasionally he tries to jump; the chain instantly brings him down again, strong as he is. If a flea be fastened to the end of an unbroken wheat straw, he will be strong enough to lift it right off the table on which it is placed. This discovery was first made by the flea proprietor, and made him turn his attention toward utilizing the race. One would think it were not difficult to procure troops of fleas, and to train them to perform; but it appears that neither task is easy. It is very difficult to procure a lot of able-bodied fleas, and it is by no means every sort of flea that will do. They must be human fleas: dog fleas, cat fleas, and bird fleas are of no use—they are not lively enough, nor strong enough, and break down soon in their training. Human fleas, therefore, must be obtained somehow, and our friend has created a market for them. The dealers who supply the raw material are principally elderly females; the trade price of fleas, moreover (like the trade price of everything else), varies, but the average price is threepence a dozen. In the wintertime it is sixpence; and, on one occasion, the trainer was obliged to give the large sum of sixpence for one single flea.* He had arranged to give a performance; the time arrived; he unpacked the fleas; one, whose presence was necessary to make up a certain number, was gone. What was to be done? The vacancy must be filled. At last, an ostler, pitying the manager's distress, supplied the needful animal; but he required sixpence for it, and sixpence he got.

While looking at the performance there came in a fresh supply of fleas, a swarm of them, in a vial bottle, huddled all together at the bottom. The flea trainer gave them a shake, and immediately they all began hopping about, hitting their horny little heads against the sides of the bottle (which was held sideways) with such force that there was a distinct noise, as if one had gently tapped the bottle with a nail. These fleas were not very good friends, for they were perpetually getting entangled in masses, and fighting with their tiny but powerful legs, and rolling over and over as if in mortal combat. They were not, however, fighting for life and death; for I did not see one that looked tired or injured after the melee.

I observed one fact, which gave me great pleasure; namely, that fleas are at enmity with bugs. There was one bug in the bottle surrounded by many fleas; the poor bug rushed continually

---

* The gentleman profiled—a Mr. Kitchingman—later wrote to Buckland to add that "In warm weather I breed fleas from the egg, the larvae feeding on the scurfy excrescence of human skin. I find these home-bred insects much more tractable." —P.C.

from one end of the bottle to the other, running the gauntlet of assembled fleas; every flea he came near attacked him; at last, the bug, overwhelmed by numbers, had the worst of it, and beat an ignoble retreat into a bit of flannel.

Fleas are not always brought to market in vial bottles. The best fleas are imported from Russia, and come over in pillboxes packed in the finest cotton wool. These fleas are big, powerful, and good workers. I wonder whether the Custom House authorities think it worthwhile to examine the contents of these pillboxes.[†] When our friend in Marylebone makes his annual tour into the provinces, his wife sends him weekly a supply of fleas in the corner of an envelope, packed in tissue paper. She is careful not to put them in the corner where the stamp goes, as the post-office clerk would, with his stamp marker, at one blow, smash the whole of the stock.

A flea cannot be taken up from its wild state and made to work at once; like a colt or puppy, it must undergo a course of training and discipline. The training is brought about as follows. The flea is taken up gently, and a noose of the finest "glass-silk" is passed round his neck, and there tied with a peculiar knot. The flea, unfortunately for himself, has a groove or depression between his neck and his body, which serves as a capital hold-fast for the bit of silk; it can slip neither up nor down, and he cannot push it off with his legs; he is a prisoner, and is thus tied to

---

[†] In recent years, artist Maria Cardoso did indeed find her flea circus blocked by Customs from entry into Britain. The Tate Modern Museum, however, proved more welcoming, and acquired one of her circuses in 2007. —P.C.

his work. This delicate operation is generally performed under a magnifying glass; but, after a time, the eye gets so accustomed to the work that the glass is not always used. In no way is the future performing flea mutilated; his kangaroolike springing legs are not cut off, nor are his lobsterlike walking legs interfered with—a flea must be in perfect health to perform well.

Every night each flea is taken out of his trappings, fed, and placed in a private compartment for the night; before they go to bed, they have their supper, and in the morning also their breakfasts; they take their meals from the hands of their owner—sometimes he has nearly all the fleas on the backs of his hands at the same moment, biting and sucking away simultaneously. For more than twenty years he has thus daily fed his fleas without any detriment to his health; the quantity of blood each flea takes away being imperceptibly small—one drop of blood, he considers, would feed a flea for many weeks; but it is the itching sensation caused by the flea cutting the skin which is unpleasant. This feeling of irritation he felt painfully when he first began to submit himself to the tender mercies of his little performers; now he is so hardened that he feels them not at all, whether biting or sucking. When, however, there are many fleas on his hands at the same time, he suffers from a sensation of great irritation all over his body, which passes away when the supper is over. He has remarked that his fleas will not feed if his hand be not kept perfectly motionless; the act, therefore, of feeding and harnessing his company of performers is troublesome, and he is obliged to devote two hours in the morning and two hours in the evening to it.

# THE MANUFACTURED
# WOMAN

**M**ermaids seem to have gone out of fashion about the same time as the dried heads of New Zealanders, but still I have been enabled to examine minutely three specimens of mermaids here in England. They are all the same in structure, and remarkable only for the ingenious way in which they have been put together. The original mermaid exhibit at the Egyptian Hall was bought for forty thousand dollars by two Italian brothers, and there was a long lawsuit about it, as there was afterward about the "Talking Fish."

There is a very capital mermaid now to be seen at the Oriental warehouse of Messrs. Farmer and Rogers, 179 Regent Street.* By the kindness of Mr. Liberty, who took the mermaid out of her case, I was enabled to examine her minutely. She certainly is a curious-looking thing; though of course to anyone with the slightest pretence to knowledge of natural history, a decided make-up.

The total length of her marine ladyship is twenty-five inches, and she is composed in the usual regulation mermaid style, viz., half fish and half quasihuman, or, as Horace says—

*Desinit in piscem mulier formosa superne.*†

The lower half of her body is made of the skin and scales of a fish of the carp family, neatly fastened onto a wooden body. The upper part of the mermaid is in the attitude of a sphinx, leaning upon its elbows and forearm. The arms are long and scraggy, and

---

* Farmer and Rogers was also notable as the best store in London for buying opium pipes. —*P.C.*
† "A woman who is beautiful above, ends in a fish's tail." —*P.C.*

the fingers are attenuated and skeleton-like. The nails are formed of little bits of ivory or bone. The head is about the size of a small orange, and the face has a laughing expression of good nature and roguish simplicity. I cannot say much for the expression of her ladyship's mouth, which is a regular gape, like the clown's mouth at a pantomime: behind her lips we see a double row of teeth, one rank being in advance of the other, like a regiment of volunteers drawn up in line. The hind teeth are conical, but the front ones project, like diminutive tusks. I am nearly as certain as I can be that these are the teeth of a young catfish—a hideous fish that one sometimes sees hanging up in the fishmongers' shops in London. Her ears are very piglike, and certainly not elegant, and her nose decidedly snub. The coiffeur is submarine, and undoubtedly *not* Parisian; it would, in fact, be no worse for a touch of the brush and comb. Mermaids in pictures generally are represented with a hand-glass and comb, as though they paid great attention to the toilet, with the openly avowed purpose, as Tennyson tells in his "Confessions of a Mermaid," that—

> All the mermen under the sea
> Would feel their immortality
> Die in the hearts for the love of me.

If I were a merman I should decidedly not fall in love with any mermaid who was not a great deal more particular in matters of hairdressing than our friend under the glass case.

At the back of her head we see a series of knobs, which run down the back till they join with a bristling row of twenty-four spines—evidently the spines of the dorsal fin of the carplike fish. The ribs in our mermaid are exceedingly prominent.

Tennyson gives an admirable description of the mermaids' submarine palace, and also of the social habits of mermaids in general:

> I would comb my hair till my ringlets would fall
> Low adown, low adown,
> From under my starry sea-bud crown
> Low adown, and around.
> And I should look like a fountain of gold
> Springing alone,
> With a shrill inner sound,
> Over the throne
> In the midst of the hall.

To judge, however, from the appearance of our Regent Street specimen, there must have been a rinderpest and famine price of provisions in general down in these splendid submarine regions, for our poor mermaid is very thin, and seems half-starved and terribly shabby, and altogether has a workhouse look about her.

In March 1866, I received the following letter from C.H., a correspondent of *Land and Water*: "Captain Cuming, R.N., of Braidwood Terrace, Plymouth, has returned from Yokohama, bringing with him a great variety of curiosities. Amongst them is a mermaid. The head is that of a small monkey, with prominent teeth; a little thin wool on the head and upper parts; long, attenuated arms and claws, below which the ribs show very distinctly; beyond these latter the skin of a fish is so neatly joined that it is hardly possible to detect where the joint is made—in fact, where the fish begins and where the monkey leaves off. The fish has large scales, spines on the back, a square tail, and appears to be a species of chub. It is quite perfect except the head, which only seems to have been removed to make the joint. Total length about sixteen inches; color of monkey, dull slate; the fish, its natural color; and the whole in excellent preservation."

Barnum has, I believe, a very good mermaid in his Museum, and he managed, he tells us, in *Barnum's Life, by Himself*, to cause a great sensation with it, although it really is, as he himself describes it, "a diminutive specimen of an ugly, dried-up, black-looking animal about three feet long. Its mouth is open, its tail turned over, and its arms thrown up, giving it the appearance of having died in great agony."

The difficulty was to get up the mermaid fever; by dint, however, of having "ten thousand mermaid pamphlets" freely distributed, and several artfully contrived innuendos inserted in the local papers, as well as by erecting huge transparencies and ably executed pictures, representing three mermaids, in the form of very beautiful young women with long flowing hair, and also a boatful of people looking at the mermaid sailing gracefully along the surface of the sea, he managed to create a sensation.‡

The mermaid painted in the pictures was, of course, the very

‡ Barnum's famous Feegee Mermaid was first acquired in 1822 by Samuel Barrett Eades, captain of a merchant ship. He'd encountered it in Batavia, and was so smitten with the ghastly little thing that he paid $5,000 to acquire it, which he financed by selling his ship—a boat which he did not in fact own. —*P.C.*

specimen which could be seen on the other side of the "Pay Here" door of the museum.

Anyhow, Barnum himself confesses in his book to have made during the first four weeks of the exhibition of his Feegee Island mermaid the sum of $864, or about £341 sterling. Bravo Barnum!

# MERMAID OIL FOR SALE

If Barnum managed to humbug the public so well, and to make such a sum of money as above related with his Feegee Mermaid, I wonder what he would have done if he had possession of my Nondescript.

I am sorry to say I can get no history of this Nondescript. I first saw him in the shop of Mr. Wareham, china curiosity-dealer, at the corner of St. Martin's Court, Leicester Square. Mr. Wareham told me he had bought it at a sale from an old gentleman who prized it amazingly, and who in his lifetime had valued it at the sum of £100. It certainly is the most extraordinary-looking thing I ever beheld, and, indeed, I am rather offended with it; when my friends come to see my private collection, I am sorry to say their attention is more taken with my hideous Nondescript than by my other specimens which I flatter myself are more valuable and interesting.

The Nondescript is about as big as a baby three months old, and, as a crusty bachelor friend of mine once said, "really very much like one."

He has wings on the tops of his shoulders like the old army aiguillettes, and there are claws on the tips and on the extreme ends of each wing: these wings are so artfully contrived that one would believe they could be opened out and unfurled like a bat's wing at any moment the creature that carried it wished to take a fly either for business or amusement.

The arms are amazingly humanlike, and look as though the dried skin had shrunk fast onto the bone; the legs also represent a similar appearance. The hands and feet are demonlike, and of a long, scraggly, merciless appearance, and each finger and toe is armed with a formidable-looking claw. The ribs project frightfully, as though the Nondescript had lately been in reduced circumstances, and had been living for some time à la malcontent. The head is about as big as a very large apple. The ears project outward and downward, like those of an African elephant. The face is wrinkled and deformed; the nose like a pig's snout; the eyes like those of a codfish; the teeth exactly the same as those in the mermaid above described—double rows in each jaw, with protruding fangs in front; and surmounting this hideous countenance, a rough shock of fine, wool-like hair, presenting the true prison convict crop, as though the Nondescript had been in trouble and had had "the key turned upon him"; and this I should think more than likely, for a more villainous-looking rascal I never beheld; a policeman would be justified in taking him up on suspicion alone.

Before this specimen came into my possession I was unable to examine it closely, as it was considered too valuable to be taken out from under the glass case. The moment, however, it came into my hands, I set to work to find out its composition. Everybody said there must be bones in the arms and legs and ribs. I soon tested this with a surgical exploring needle, but found no bone, nor anything like a bone, but simply soft wood, probably cedar. I made several incisions in the Nondescript's body, and found that the main portion of his composition was (like the legs) a light wood. The skin, as well as the wings, are made of a species of papier-mâché, most artfully put on in wrinkles, and admirably colored and shaded to give the appearance of the dried body of some creature that had once existed either on land or sea, had been slain, and then preserved as a curiosity.

Although I can obtain no history of my Nondescript, I fancy that he must be the handiwork of some ingenious Japanese. I imagine he is an ancient specimen, and has doubtless seen a great many curious adventures, if he could only tell us his history. He may possibly have been made by the very Japanese fisherman whose acquaintance Dr. Von Siebold, the well-known traveler, made in Japan, and of which he gives us an account in his work *On the Manner and Customs of the Japanese in the Nineteenth Century*. Von Siebold says:

This fisherman displayed his ingenuity by making money out of his countrymen's passion for whatever is odd and strange. He contrived to unite the upper half of a monkey to the lower half of a fish, so neatly as to defy ordinary inspection. He then gave out that he had caught the creature alive in his net, but that it had died shortly after being taken out of the water; and he derived considerable pecuniary profit from his devil in more ways than one. The exhibition of the sea-monster to Japanese curiosity paid well; but yet more productive was the assertion that the half-human fish had spoken during the few minutes it existed outside of its natural element, predicting a certain number of years of wonderful fertility, to be followed by a fatal epidemic, the only remedy against which would be possession of the marine-prophet's likeness. The sale of these pictured mermaids was immense. Either this composite animal, or another, was sold to the Dutch factory and transmitted to Batavia, where it fell into the hands of a shrewd American, who brought it to Europe; and there, in the year 1822–23, exhibited his purchase as a real mermaid at every capital—to the admiration of the ignorant, the perplexity of the learned, and the filling of his own purse.

Thus, then, we have good evidence of a regular manufactory for "Mermaids," "Nondescripts," and all such "Curioes," as my friend Robinson Crusoe would call them. The days of mermaids are now past, though the time was (judging from old books of natural history) when they were much prized and looked upon as a distinct kind of existing creatures.

There is an old proverb that there is "never smoke without fire," and I believe that the origin of the idea of the existence of mermaids and mermen was the fact of sailors having observed those semicetaceous creatures, Dugongs and Manatees.

The Indian Dugong (*Halecore Dugang*), is found round about the shores of the Indian Ocean and Ceylon; the Manatee is described by Mr. Wallace as particularly abundant in the lakes of the Amazon. These curious creatures, when diving and playing about in the water, have a very human appearance; judging from the skulls, the face is like that of a man with a long nose. Sailors, with their well-known ability of telling yarns to their friends at home, would not have much difficulty in converting a Dugong or Manatee into a real merman.

A Dugong (*Halecore Australis*) is also found on the coast of Australia, and I learn from an article from the pen of P.L. Symonds, Esquire, editor of that most useful periodical the *Technologist*, that Dr. Hobbs, a practitioner of Moreton Bay and health officer of Brisbane, Queensland, has brought Dugong oil into notice as a substitute for cod liver oil. This Dugong oil is described as equally efficacious as cod liver oil in the treatment of consumption, &c., and it has all the therapeutic effects of cod liver oil without its nauseous taste and smell.[*][†] Thus, then, we practical folks of the present day no longer make a wonder of the mermen and mermaids, but simply harpoon them and boil them down for oil for the benefit of our patients and invalid friends and relations.

---

[*] C.E. Batt writes, in *Land and Water*: "Dugong oil was introduced into England five or six years ago, but its use has been almost entirely discontinued, possibly on account of its high price, 20s. per pint. Messrs. J. Bell & Co., 338 Oxford Street, have a large stock of it on hand at the present time."

[†] Also sometimes used as a cooking oil, Dugong oil's high price may have been due to the decimation by the 1870s of herds by the Dugong-oil industry. They were nearly wiped out again by hungry Japanese garrisons in World War II. —*P.C.*

# PETRIFIED!

About five or six years ago an exhibition of a "Marble Lady" was opened at the Egyptian Hall, Piccadilly. The advertisement, in the usual flowing terms, described it as "one of the most marvelous of natural curiosities," &c. "The figure of the lady, the bonnet, parasol, gloves, &c., could all be seen exactly according to nature," &c.

I inspected it immediately, and found the "Marble Lady" carefully covered over with a velvet cloth, and otherwise protected from injury. I at once saw that it was simply a block of common black marble, about a foot square, in the center of which there was embedded a bit of fossil coral—madrepore of a white color. The exhibitor pointed out the dress (this antediluvian lady wore no crinoline), the parasol, gloves, bonnet, &c.

The worthy man was evidently fully convinced of the reality of his prize, and I could hardly make up my mind to undeceive him. At length I ventured to express my opinion as to its real nature, at which he lost his temper and showed symptoms of unmistakable anger; so I refrained from pressing my theory too far, as it was impossible to convince him of his mistake.

I hear that, in a cave somewhere in Wales, is shown a "Petrified Lady and Her Dog." This is, probably, some stalagmite, formed by the water dripping from the roof of the cave. I should much like to know where this "Petrified Lady" can be seen.*

---

* Stories of mysterious petrifactions were in vogue throughout the nineteenth century. One 1859 San Francisco *Alta* article claimed a local prospector had dropped dead upon drinking fluid he'd found inside a geode, with an autopsy subsequently finding his stomach and blood vessels all turned to stone, and his heart resembling a

In September 1863, I obtained leave of absence from my medical duties as Assistant Surgeon of the 2nd Life Guards, and made the town of Knaresborough my headquarters during my short holiday. At first sight, Knaresborough did not promise at all well, but eventually I found that there was "sport" to be had, as the following few pages will show.

My first visit was to the well-known dropping well. I entered the enclosure where it is situated with a certain amount of fear, lest I myself should in a moment be converted into stone by this modern wholesale statue-maker; but I summoned up courage and knocked at the door. It was opened by a civil Yorkshire lassie, and we saw before us this natural curiosity—a massive frowning rock, over which a perpetual shower of water fell incessantly, with a musical and somewhat melancholy sound, into the clear pool below. About halfway down, on the face of the rock, were suspended a number of curious-looking objects. I asked the girl to explain them. Pointing to them, she at once began with a true Yorkshire accent and with wonderful volubility of tongue—

"There you will see a pumkin and a stocking—a squirrel and a stock dove—a small hotter, and a nedgeog [hedgehog]—a branch and a pheasant—a man's hat and a sponge—a moss basket and a bird's nest—a weasel and a wig."

"For goodness' sake, my girl, gently, gently, give us the list over again," but she was gone, other visitors had knocked at the

---

piece of red jasper. A related humbug was "toad in the hole," or ancient amphibians allegedly found alive deep inside boulders and seams of coal. —*P.C.*

door; they also came down to where we were standing, and the girl began again, "a pumkin and a stocking, a small hotter and a nedgeog," down to the wig at the end of the sentence.

"Where's my dog?" said my friend.

"He is gone," said the girl. "We wants a curly dog, and if I catch him, I'll just hang him oop in t'well and petrify him."

Poor Brittle had evidently taken warning from the fate of the "small hotter and a nedgeog," and had fairly bolted for it, his tail between his legs, lest he should be "hung oop" and become petrified.

The girl did not seem to know much more about the well than the names of the things hung up to petrify, so we left her and looked about for ourselves.

The rocks about Knaresborough are composed of magnesian limestone, and the lime becomes dissolved in the spring water—so highly charged, indeed, is it with mineral matter, that in a gallon of water there are of carbonate of lime twenty-three parts, sulphate of magnesia eleven parts, and sulphate of lime 132 parts, and a pint of it weighs twenty-four grams heavier than one of common water.

The water seems willing enough to get rid of its mineral burden, and anything, therefore, placed within its reach, so to say, it converts into stone. This is not, however, actually the case; they are merely covered over with a coating of stonelike material, which, of course, takes the form of the objects which it encrusts. I have now before me a moorhen and a "nedgeog" from the well at Knaresborough. The form of these creatures is not, as may be imagined, very well preserved. The hedgehog reminds one much of the hedgehogs made of sponge cake which one sees in the pastry cook's shop. I have made a section of my fossil moorhen, and found the stony coating very hard indeed, and much like in appearance, as indeed it is in composition, to the fur which is found inside ordinary teakettles. The feathers, bones, &c. of the birds have almost disappeared from decay. The cast, however, of it is accurately taken by the deposit from the well. I have also a wig, but this is a terribly shapeless mass, and very fragile. In the showroom of the hotel by the cave are many really beautiful specimens of incrustations, particularly the birds' nests and a pheasant, of which the form is accurately preserved. There is also a badger, which would form an excellent museum specimen, for the traces of the rough hair are distinctly perceptible, even though it is one solid mass of stone. I have also a bird's nest or two with the eggs in them. Both eggs and nests are hard and solid—in fact, a perfect mass of heavy stone, and very pretty ornaments for the drawing room they are. I have broken one of these eggs, and find the eggshell bright and white inside its stonelike cover.

We crept about under the deep ledges of the rock, and found ample proofs of the wonderful Medusalike power of this water. A mass of leaves, moss, sticks, &c. had evidently, at some time, been blown together by the wind up in the corner where we found them. We could see the individual leaves, moss, branches, &c. as plain as though they had just been brought there, but when I attempted to remove a leaf—no; it was hard, firm, fixed as solid as a wreath carved on a marble tombstone. A most beautiful group of natural objects was this; and much more striking than the hideous outstretched and deformed worsted stocking we saw hung up under the well.

This process of nature-casting has been taken advantage of by the art-loving Italians. At San Filippo, between Rome and Sienna, there is also a dripping well, but the deposit in this case is white, like marble. The proprietors, wishing to turn this natural manufactory to account, have placed under the drip molds and medallions of antique heads, figures, &c. made of sulphur. The water, careless of results, artistic or not, has deposited carbonate of lime on the molds to the thickness of half an inch or more, taking a most beautifully accurate cast of the figure *in rilievo*, the surface being very smooth and polished, answering to the surface of the sulphur. This deposit goes on so gradually, and with such minuteness, that even the lines in a delicate wood engraving have been accurately molded, and we have the picture in hard, solid carbonate of lime, instead of thin, perishable paper. If we reverse one of these stone pictures we shall find that the outside layer is exceedingly rough and indented, the results of the water dripping from the well. I have a case containing a number of these beautiful casts, brought by the Dean from Italy, and they are, I believe, almost unique in this country. I wish the worthy proprietor of the Mother Shipton, the hotel[†] at

---

† Mother Shipton's Cave and Petrifying Well is still open, and if you are willing to part with £5, you may witness what teddy bears look like after petrifaction. Those with a more antiquarian bent may note a top hat abandoned by a Victorian contemporary of Buckland's. It is now fused solid into the well. —*P.C.*

Knaresborough on the grounds of which the dropping well is situated, would take the hint above given, and endeavor to cause his well to set to work, and become a candidate for a prize in the School of Design department of the South Kensington Museum.

# THE GROWING PLATE

I n February 1860, the following advertisement appeared in the *Times*:

GO AND SEE MR. HENRY HEALEY'S GROWING PLATE.—The most wonderful natural phenomenon of the age. The surface of an old china dinner plate, which has been in the possession of Mr. H's family for nearly three hundred years, during which long period it has escaped the accidents of time, is now covered with eruptions of the purest crystal, resembling palaces, shrubs, flowers, &c., of the most exquisite beauty. On the 8th of August, 1859, it was removed from the cupboard for ordinary purposes, when it was found to be covered with small eruptions, which created much surprise, and being preserved, has continued to develop its wonderful natural curiosities to the present time. The attention of antiquarians and men of science is expressly invited. Now on view at 147 Oxford Street, opposite New Bond Street. Admission 1s.

I at once paid a visit to this wonderful plate. It was placed on a pedestal, with a glass shade over it and a railing round it. At first sight, one would imagine that bits of common washing soda had been scattered over the plate, and attached to it by gum; but, on closer inspection with a magnifying glass, I observed numerous excrescences of a whitish opaque substance, apparently growing or extending themselves out of the center and rim of the plate, each supporting upon its surface a portion of the actual enamel of the plate.

The largest eruption (if it may be so called) is about the size and shape of a fourpenny bit, and it has raised up a portion of enamel above the surface of the plate to about the height represented by the thickness of a new penny-piece. In another place is seen a portion of enamel, also of an oblong shape, just being raised up above its ordinary level by the substance which is coming up from below. Numerous minor eruptions are also seen in the plate, all presenting the same appearance, viz., that of some substance taking its origin from the interspace between the upper and lower surfaces of the plate, each raising with it a portion of enamel corresponding in size to the extruding material.

I have not the least doubt that it is a natural production; that the material is of mineral parasitic growth, resulting from some chemical decomposition of the clay with which the plate was originally formed.

My friend Warrington Smyth, Esquire, of the Government School of Mines, has kindly written me the following opinion on this point:

> I wish, for the sake of a solution to your question about the growing plate, you had been able to obtain a bit of that famous piece of crockery. But in the absence of opportunity for testing it, I have little doubt that its "growth" must have been analogous to the fibrous shoots of ice which you may see on a frosty morning, bearing upon them bits of earth or little stones, which they have raised from the ground with the force developed in crystallizations. In the old workings of the mines,

the vigorous extension of acicular crystals of sundry salts (such as sulphates of alumina, of magnesia, or of iron) appear under very similar aspects, and often look exceedingly like vegetation. The efflorescence of salts in alluvial plains—as in Hungary and Egypt—is of the same kind. Now, the body of the plate contains alumina, sometimes magnesia, and sundry hypotheses might be started for bringing to these bases the necessary sulphuric acid for forming the fibrous crystals of alum[*] or Epsom salt, which I fancy was most likely the growing part of the plate, which carried upon its crest the fragments of the broken glaze.

Yours, very truly,

WARRINGTON SMYTH.

The proprietor told me that he had refused a cheque of £1,000 for his specimen. I therefore advise my readers to look in their china closets, and see if any of their plates have *grown* since they were deposited there.

---

[*] Buckland was viewing this plate at the studio of London photographer William Kent. Curiously, alum is a vital chemical in photography. —*P.C.*

Upon entering the room at St. James's Hall, in company with my friend H.J.B. Hancock, Esquire, in order to examine this "wonder of the world," as the proprietor calls his mechanical vocalist, a paper was placed in my hands, stating that the Anthropoglossos would sing the following songs: "The Dark Girl Dressed in Blue," "Polly Perkins," "Annie Lyle," "God Bless the Prince of Wales," &c., &c. We were informed that "the words of each song would be distinctly articulated," and that "never since the first sound of the human voice emanated from the earliest created of mankind, calling the oral mystery of sounding syllables that float upon the balmy airs of Paradise, until now, had aught been perfected which could approximate, in any degree, to the divinely bestowed music of speech, and that the automaton head could rival Nature herself in its vocal elocutionary powers."

We observed two huge wax heads at each end of a platform, ghastly and lifeless, like the heads of executed criminals; and just behind a railing a gigantic wax head, which is evidently meant to be a portrait of Jullien, but which rather reminded me of the head of the giant Goliath, as seen in the picture galleries in the hands of David. As we entered, the head was singing "Annie Lyle," and the visitors were passing in single file in front of the railing, each stopping for a moment to look at the funnel which came out of the head's mouth, and whence the voice was supposed to issue.

"Uncommonly human, that voice," said I to my friend; "it is *too good*, and the thing has been overdone. There is, moreover, nothing metallic whatever about the voice, and I should not be the least surprised to hear it cough or sneeze; but, however, let us take our places."

As we advanced nearer the head, we observed that it was supported by two brass chains from above, and was in no way connected with any tube or pipe, but, like Mohammed's coffin, hung suspended in midair. The voice was supposed to come from the funnel which projected from the automaton's mouth. Beneath the head, however, was a sort of petticoat or frock, in which was contained the mechanism, which was regularly wound up, music-box fashion, when the song was about to commence.*

My friend, myself, and another friend who happened to be present reasoned thus: if the voice comes from the funnel, there must be a draft of air; let us try the experiment. We therefore, having no light feather or other substance suited for the purpose, each cut off the ends of a silk cord inside our hats, and with a penknife spread them out into the finest possible fibers, so that they would show the least puff of air.

My turn arriving, I marched boldly up and placed my "vocometer" (if I may coin a word) into the automaton's funnel; but no—not the least motion or draft of air was perceptible! Then followed my friend with his tuft of silk, and another accurate observer brought up the rear, each testing for themselves.

On comparing notes, we found that all three of our tufts

---

* A similar suspended singing box, dubbed "The Invisible Girl," was featured at Mrs. Salmon's Waxworks at 17 Fleet Street many decades earlier. —P.C.

of silk, when placed in the funnel, had been equally *unmoved*, though the head been singing gaily all the time.

While we were talking, we heard the sound of a scuffle behind us, and also the sound of a blow given. It appeared that a gentleman who had come to examine the instrument had placed his pocket handkerchief over a piece of perforated zinc which was let into the railing in front of the head, and that the person in charge of the head had taken the law into his own hands and struck out at him, accusing him of trying to turn the head round and injure it.

Both my friends and myself formed our own opinions, which are decidedly not favorable to the metal mechanism of the voice we heard; particularly as, alas! the Anthropoglossos *clipped* his H's.

# DEAD FOLK AT PLAY

Waxen images of persons seem somehow or another to have fallen into disrepute. For my own part, if wax can be used to preserve the likeness of a person, I do not see why it should not be as highly esteemed as marble. I suppose it is not much thought of because of the waxen heads of ladies with long hair we see in the barbers' shops. Waxen babies, pigs, ears, hands, arms, eyes, noses, &c. are hung up as ex-votos at the present day in churches in France.

I have examined very carefully the oldest waxworks in England. These, I hardly need say, are the waxworks in Westminster Abbey, and which to my mind are national relics worthy of the greatest respect and reverence. The following account is given in a description of the Abbey, its monuments and curiosities, printed by "J. Newberry, at the Bible and Sun, in St. Paul's Churchyard, 1754." In this curious pamphlet, the Westminster Abbey waxworks are called the "Play of the Dead Folks" and the "Ragged Regiment."*

The following is the account of the condition of these waxworks one hundred and twenty years ago:

> Over this chapel (Islip, otherwise St. Erasmus) is a chantry, in which are two large wainscot-presses, full of the effigies of princes and others of high quality buried in the Abbey. These effigies resembled the deceased as nearly as possible, and were wont to be exposed at the funerals of our princes and other great personages in open chariots, with the proper

---

* For many years, monks of the abbey staged "Ragged Regiment" and "Play of the Dead Folks" waxwork sideshows to supplement their income. —P.C.

ensigns of royalty or honor attended. Those that are here laid up are in a sad mangled condition, some stripped and others in tattered robes, but all maimed or broken. The most ancient are the least injured, by which it would seem as if the costliness of their clothes had occasioned the ravage; for the robes of Edward VI, which were once of crimson velvet, but now appear like leather, are left entire; but those of Queen Elizabeth and King James I are entirely stripped, as are all the rest of anything of value. In two handsome wainscot-presses are the effigies of King William and Queen Mary and Queen Anne in good condition, and greatly admired by every eye that beholds them.

The figure of Cromwell is not here mentioned, but in the account of his lying in state the effigy is described as made to the life in wax, appareled in velvet, gold lace, and ermine. "This effigy was laid upon the bed of state, and carried upon the hearse in funeral procession; both were then deposited in Westminster Abbey; but at the Restoration the hearse was broken in pieces, and the effigies was destroyed after hanging from a window in Whitehall."

When my father was the Dean of Westminster, somehow or other he seldom used to show visitors to the Abbey into the curious room, and it is now only to be seen by special order from the Dean. The visitor ascends through a timeworn staircase into the chapel, and a most curious sight then meets his eye. Set up against the wall are very large, massive cases, not unlike big clock cases. There are glasses in front of them, so that the figures inside can be well seen. As far as I could see, they are not labelled except with chalk superscriptions.

Dr. Stanley, Dean of Westminster, has, in his most interesting *Memorials of Westminster Abbey* (Murray, 1868), p. 340, the following able observations on these waxworks:

> The "lively effigy" was a practice which has its precedent, if not its origin, in the funerals of the great men of the Roman Commonwealth. The one distinguishing mark of a Roman noble was the right of having figures with waxen masks, representing his ancestors, carried at his obsequies and placed in his hall.
>
> In England the royal funerals were, till the time of Henry V, distinguished by the exhibition of the corpse itself of the deceased sovereign. But even before that time the practice of effigies had been adopted.
>
> These wax figures were detached from the hearses and kept in the Abbey, generally near the graves of the deceased, but were gradually drafted off into wainscot presses above the Islip Chapel. Here they were seen in Dryden's time—
>
> > And now the presses open stand,
> > And you may see them all a-row.
>
> In 1658 the following were the waxen figures thus exhibited:
>
> > Henry the Seventh and his fair Queen,
> > Edward the First and his Queen,
> > Henry the Fifth here stands upright,

And his fair Queen was this Queen,

The noble Prince, Prince Henry,

King James's eldest son,

King James, Queen Anne, Queen Elizabeth.

And so this chapel's done.

With this agrees the curious notice of them in 1708:

And so we went on to see the ruins of majesty in
the waxen figures placed there by authority. As
soon as we had ascended half a score stone steps in
a dirty, cobwebbed hole, and in old, worm-eaten
presses, whose doors flew open at our approach,
here stood Edward III as they told us, which was a
broken piece of waxwork, a battered head, a straw-
stuffed body, not one-quarter covered with rags. [†]
His beautiful queen stood by, not better in repair;
and so, the number of half a score kings and queens,
not near so good a figure as the King of the Beggars
would make, and all the begging crew would be
ashamed of their company. The rear was brought up
with Good Queen Bess, with the remnants of an old
dirty ruff, and nothing else to cover her.

---

[†] It was not unknown for the castoff old garments of royalty to eventually make
their way into London theatrical wardrobes. John Smith's *A Book for a Rainy Day*
(1845) recalled a grand old wig of Charles II that was gleefully requisitioned by one
comic actor; when he wore it on stage, "sick men laughed themselves well to see him
peeping out the black forest of hair." —*P.C.*

But there are eleven figures in a tolerable state of preservation. That of Queen Elizabeth was, as we have seen, already worn out in 1708, and the existing figure is, doubtless, the one made by order of the chapter to commemorate the bicentenary of the foundation of the Collegiate Church in 1760. As late as 1783 it stood in Henry VII's chapel. The effigy of Charles II used to stand over his grave, and close beside him that of General Monk. The former is tolerably perfect, and seems to have early attracted from the contrast with his battered predecessors. Monk used to stand beside his monument by Charles II's grave. The effigy is in too dilapidated a condition to be shown, but the remnants of his armor exist still. The famous cap, in which the contributions for the showmen were collected, is gone.

The effigy to which I made my bow was King Charles II, dressed in magnificent raiment. The wax of the face is somewhat bleached by the sun, but I should imagine from the pictures that the portrait is exceedingly good. The robes must have once been very grand; the lace on the king's breast is of the finest Venetian point. The king has long black hair; he was evidently a dark-looking man, but one expects that at any moment his features will break out into a jovial smile. King Charles died in A.D. 1685—nearly two hundred years ago. If this is the original effigy used at his funeral, it has lasted very well indeed.

# THE BONE CENSUS

The object of my visit to Ripon Cathedral was to examine the collection of human bones which I had heard were preserved in a crypt there. Such collections of human remains should always be regarded with a proper amount of reverence, considering their sacred nature; but there is, nevertheless, no reason why we should not inquire into their nature and history, particularly when it is obscure.

Leaving the ancient chapter house, Mr. Benson, the civil and intelligent verger, conducted us to the crypt, which is underneath it. Unlocking the massive door, we at once beheld a Golgotha. Bones, bones, bones everywhere: arm bones, leg bones, skulls of old men, young men, men in the prime of life, and of women and children; they were not, I am pleased to say, in an unseemly and incongruous mass, but all stacked and arranged with decency and order. So many bones are there that the visitor cannot see the walls of the crypt, for against them is piled a wall of bones about six feet high, and four feet in thickness. Considerable taste (if I may use the expression) has been exhibited in the arrangement of the bones. In former times they were all scattered in confusion about the vault, but the old sexton of the parish, Mr. Dennis Wilson (himself now resting in the quiet churchyard), undertook, in 1843, much to his credit, the task of arranging them. He placed a row of skulls on the floor; then a thick row of arm and leg bones with the round ends protruding; then another layer of skulls, and so on, till the space from the floor to the roof of the crypt was entirely occupied. I counted these skulls in their several compartments, and found that there were, from the wall to the outside of the stack, thirteen skulls in a row, and twelve in a row lengthways.*

I remarked great variety in the conformation of the skulls. Some were long and narrow, others broad and massive; some were bulletheaded, some deliberately shaped and classical; some presented the orbits of the eyes open and well marked, in others they were peeping and diminutive. In some the teeth were good, in others bad. Few of these bones or skulls presented any signs of decay, the vault being excessively dry. Then again, the pillars of the crypt were ornamented with festoons of skulls. The arches from the pillars to the walls sustained rows of skulls; in fact, wherever there was a vacant space there was a skull placed. One of the skulls, in particular, presented a highly polished surface on the forehead. This I think can be accounted for by the fact that this skull happens to be just in the place most easily reached by the hand of the visitor, and the touch of the fingers of many visitors for years past has given it this peculiar appearance.† I am more convinced of this because an enormously long femur, or thigh bone, is kept separate from the rest, and is placed in the hands of the visitors by the verger for examination. This femur carries a bright polish, like a looking glass.‡ The thigh bone of

---

* One famously narrow passage in this crowded crypt, Wilfrid's Needle, could traditionally only be squeezed through by virgins. —P.C.

† The toe of a statue in St. Paul's Cathedral presents the same polished appearance. A couplet, written by the late Phil. Duncan, Esquire, runs thus: "And the lips of the pilgrims devout / Have kissed off St. Peter's toe."

‡ That bones will take a high polish is evident from the appearance of the bones used by cobblers in finishing off their work. I have in my collection a specimen

my friend Mr. Joseph Brice, the French giant, was twenty-two-and-a-half inches in length: we may, therefore, possibly conclude that the man of whose body this Ripon bone formed a part approximated to the same height as Brice. I also observed among the arm and leg bones several cases of fracture, and subsequent reparation, showing that surgery in some parts of Ripon's ancient history was not at its maximum of perfection.

I was curious to arrive at some sort of idea of the number of human beings represented by the bones in this crypt. Each person must of necessity have had a skull, so that, by counting the skulls, I conceived I might get at an approach to the number of people whose remains were deposited in this crypt. We accordingly counted the skulls in their length, breadth, and thickness; measured the compartments, length of the crypt, &c., and, by a calculation, we made out that there were the skulls of about 9,912 persons in these bone stacks in the crypt. Not all of the bones of these individuals were, of course, there, as there would not have been room for them. All other bones of the skeletons, save and except the skulls and the arm and leg bones, the verger had buried in the churchyard at the time he stacked them. "But you must go on with your calculations, sir," said the verger. "Why so?" I asked. "Because," said he, "underneath the floor of the crypt is another mass of bones, buried under the ground on which you now tread;

---

showing this fact well. It is the metacarpal bone, about nine inches long, of a cow. I bought it from a weaver at Knaresborough, who told me it had been in use for more than one hundred and fifty years. One half of the bone is entirely worn away; the whole surface presents a lustrous polish.

they are also stacked, and are four feet in thickness, and are spread all over the walls of the crypt."** What a vast assemblage of the mortal remains of human beings are, therefore, collected together! I leave it for the reader to calculate the sum.

---

** These skulls might be ancient indeed. Ripon has England's oldest crypt, remaining from a church built in 672 A.D. by St. Wilfrid, patron saint of bakers. —P.C.

# THE SINISTER COTTAGE

When doing my duty as Medical Officer in charge of the 2nd Life Guards in Aldershot Camp, in June 1861, our Regimental Quartermaster, Corporal Major Waite, knowing my love for curious things, was good enough to bring me a copy of the *Aldershot Gazette*, in which I read the following:

REMARKABLE DISCOVERY AT ALDERSHOT.—On Monday morning, some workmen who were removing earth near the Royal Horse Artillery barracks, South Camp, Aldershot, discovered the skull of a person who had evidently met with a violent death many years ago. The skull, which appeared to be that of a full-grown man, was pierced at the top with a gunshot wound, and there was a slug wound in one of the eyes, with the slug remaining in it. A part of the jawbone seemed to have rotted away, and a surgeon gave it as his opinion that the skull had been in the ground twelve or fourteen years or less. The present site of the camp was a wild heath a few years ago, and the neighborhood is associated with many tales of the exploits of highwaymen. No other remnants of a human being, except the skull, were found by the workmen, and that has been placed in the hands of the police, who are instituting inquiries respecting it.

I immediately got on my horse and rode away up to the South Camp, where I found the good folks in a considerable state of excitement about the matter, and this made me more anxious than ever to see and examine the skull. At last, by the kindness of a brother Medical Officer, I was enabled to examine it, and make inquiries about it. It appeared that some of the troopers of the Horse Artillery, when hunting for rats at the back of their stables in the camp, turned up this skull; they could not imagine how it got there. The fact was, therefore, reported to the police, and, according to the *Aldershot Gazette*, "the skull was taken to the Coroner." There was a hole on the top of the skull, which was made by the point of a pitchfork by the sergeant who found it; there was, besides, the mark of a cut or wound in the bone over the right eye—this wound had healed over, and must therefore have been inflicted some years before death; there was also a small leaden bullet, such as would be fired from a revolver, still fixed in the bone of the outer wall of the orbit of the left eye. From the situation of this leaden bullet it was probable that the shot had been fired from behind the victim.

Of course everybody said there had been a murder committed at some time or another; and following the hint thrown out by the *Aldershot Gazette*, the prevailing idea was that some unfortunate traveler had been shot by a highwayman upon Aldershot heath in the "good old days" when highwaymen abounded upon this abominable desert heath—I call it abominable because soldiering and perpetual Regimental "Field Days" in this bleak wilderness are not at all suited to my taste. Anyhow, there was a considerable "talkee, talkee" about the skull—murder, pistols, Dick Turpin, highwaymen, &c. There was, however, an awkward little fact that nobody could account for, viz., where was the rest of the poor murdered man's body? Only the skull was found; what could the highwayman have done with the body of his victim? Nobody could explain that; yet here was the skull, and the skull only, to be accounted for. At length (and I was really in one way very sorry for it, for it stopped all the speculations, the inquiries of the sagacious police, the coroner's inquest, &c., &c.) the mystery was explained in the most prosaic way possible.

It turned out that a sergeant of the Chestnut troop of the Royal Horse Artillery had received the skull as a present from the servant of Captain ——, *who had brought it from the Crimea.* The sergeant's wife did not approve of the skull being in such close proximity to her domestic arrangements in her husband's hut while in camp, so in order to put it out of the way of his better half, the sergeant buried it about one foot deep in the ground in the rear of the stables. He intended, I believe, when the time came for the regiment to move from the camp into town quarters, to have dug up the skull and taken it with him. However, fate decreed otherwise.

If the sergeant had not very properly and credibly come forward to explain how this skull came to be deposited in the place where it was found, it is probable that much more would have been said and done about it than *was* said and done.

I was very anxious to obtain the skull, which had caused so much discussion in the camp, and the brother Medical Officer above mentioned was good enough to give it to me. The sergeant, having had more bother with it than was agreeable—first with his wife, and then with the stir and fuss made among the soldiers about its discovery—was pleased to get rid of it.

It is now on the shelves of my museum at Albany Street; but I am sorry to say I have lost the bullet out of it.

As soon as I had an opportunity, after returning from the camp, I took it to the Royal College of Surgeons and compared it with the other skulls in the ethnological section of this magnificent collection. It appeared to me, and to other medical friends who were with me, that this cranium found at Aldershot must be, as it is reported to be, a Russian. The peculiar round shape of the head, the formation of the cheekbones and forehead, as well as other points, led us to this conclusion. It is, moreover, a smaller head than the generality of the European type; this may or may not be an individual peculiarity of the cranium; anyhow, all the Russian helmets I have seen seem to have been made for people with small heads.

Although this skull turned out after all to be the skull of a Russian brought from the Crimea, the matter set us all talking about highwaymen, &c.; and in the course of conversation, an Officer told me of a discovery of human remains which it is not at all improbable were really those of some unfortunate murdered traveler. During some excavations in front of the south cavalry barracks at the camp, the workmen came upon a mass of lime three or four feet beneath the surface; and in this lime were concealed the remains of a human being. The outline of the body was apparent, as well as a portion of the skull, ethmoid, and metacarpal bones; all the rest was converted into the waxlike substance which is called adipocere.* The next day the bones of a horse were discovered only a few yards away from the spot where the human remains had been

---

* Also known as *mortuary fat* and *grave wax*, adipocere is, in effect, the posthumous conversion of body fat into soap. —*P.C.*

buried. The horse's bones were in good preservation, and no lime had been placed on them. The spot where these skeletons were found was situated outside the hedge of what had formerly been a lone cottage, not far from the high road; no records of any kind were found with them, nor are there any local traditions as to how this man and horse came to be buried in the out-of-the-way place. May it not be fairly imagined that some foul deed had taken place here in former times—some poor traveler entrapped into the house and murdered—his horse shot, and both buried—the man without a coffin, in lime, in order to get rid of the body, the horse without lime, as its bones would not cause suspicion if discovered?

Upon inquiry I learned that several stories of highwaymen's deeds on Aldershot and Bagshot heaths are still recollected by the inhabitants of the neighborhood. There is a small wayside public house at the village of Hale, between Aldershot camp and the town of Farnham, which is pointed out as the site of the escape of Dick Turpin through its back windows. The landlord of the Cricketer's Arms, near Bagshot, told me that the lone public house on the top of Bagshot Hill was formerly called the "Golden Farmer" (it is now the "Jolly Farmer"), and was presided over by a highwayman, or else a fellow in league with the highwaymen.[†] Just beyond the Golden Farmer is a lane called to this day Gibbet

---

† Specifically, the highwayman William Davies, a master of disguise who once donned an outfit to rob his own unwitting landlord shortly after paying the rent. After decades of crime, Davies was caught and hung in 1690. The Jolly Farmer survived as a pub into the postwar era, but today is the site of the American Discount Golf Store. —P.C.

Lane, as a man formerly hung in chains at the point where it joins the road.‡ An ancient postboy died at Staines not many months ago, who remembered affrays with highwaymen, and who bore the marks on his crippled foot of a bullet shot at him by one of these worthies, whose genus is now, thank goodness, extinct.

I recollect my mother telling me that, when she was a little girl, traveling over this very heathland in her annual visit to London with her father, she used to wear a bonnet the lining of which was stuffed with bank notes for fear of the highwaymen. It has been recommended by an authority that when modern travelers are journeying in suspicious, out-of-the-way places on the continent, &c., they should sew up sovereigns in the buttons of their coats, and so carry them without suspicion.** But, say

---

‡ Our ancestors were not over-particular about their medicines, for according to Pomet's *History of Drugs*, 1712, you may see in the druggists' shops of London skulls covered with moss, and some that only have the moss growing on some parts. This moss is called usnea, because of its near resemblance to the moss that grows upon oaks; it is found on the heads of men that have long hung in gibbets, and the like. The English druggists generally bring these heads from Ireland, that country having been remarkable for them since the "Irish Massacre." This moss was used in the composition of the "sympathetick ointment," available in cure of "falling sickness."

** The Victorian rogue Baron Nicholson took advantage of this well-known ploy when apprenticing for a pawnbroker: "When a queer old second-hand jacket, which would really not fit anyone, was in stock, the common practice was to pick open the breast of it, and place therein four or five farthings, then carefully stitch them over, as if they had been [gold coins] placed there by the previous owner for secrecy and safety. Ludicrous indeed were these sales. A sailor, feeling the suppositious sovereigns... would insist on making the purchase, without any regard to the shape, make, or fit of the garment. To see a big fellow in a boy's jacket, and to watch him run down the nearest court or alley, and witness his eagerness to rip up the lining to get at the concealed treasure, was great fun." —*P.C.*

I, this plan won't do, for *where would be the traveler if somebody should walk off with his coat?*

Mr. Galton, in his *Art of Travel*, under the heading "Secreting Jewels," says "Before going among a rich but semi-civilized people, travelers sometimes buy a few small jewels, and shut them up into a little silver tube with rounded edges; then, making a gash in their skin, they bury it there, allowing the flesh to heal over it. They feel no inconvenience from its presence, any more than a once-wounded man does from a bullet lodged in his person, or from a plate of silver set beneath the scalp. The best place for burying it is on the left arm, at the spot chosen for vaccination. By this means, should a traveler be robbed of everything, he could still fall back on his jewels. I fear, however, that if his precious depot were suspected, any robbers whose hands he may fall into would fairly mince him to pieces in search of further treasures." That this barbarous practice was once in vogue, we learn from Josephus, who then described "the great slaughters and sacrilege that were in Jerusalem," tells us "that the Jews who deserted from the besieged city were in the habit of swallowing gold coins. The camp followers of the Roman army killed these unfortunate men for the sake of the money they might contain."

Relative to the discovery of skulls, my friend Mr. Bush tells me a capital story. When in practice as a medical man at Witney, in Oxfordshire, he, one day, as he was going his morning's round, met the coroner on his way to hold an inquest. The coroner told him that the head and bones of a child had been found at —— village, and that a woman was suspected of having committed a murder and concealed the body of her infant. A sudden thought struck Mr. Bush that he would like to accompany the coroner and attend the inquest, and fortunate it was for the poor woman that he did so. On his arrival at the cottage, the head and bones were brought out with due form and solemnity, while a crowd of gaping villagers stood chattering at the door. At first sight of the bones, Mr. Bush said, "Well, it's all clear about these bones, anyhow: they are rabbit's bones; there are the leg bones, and there are the blade bones, &c. They are not human bones at all; but as for the child's head, I don't know what to say about that." An old woman volunteered as evidence that Mr. —— had been there and examined it, and given it as his opinion that it was a child's head or *summut*.††

The shape of it was amazingly like an infant's head; yet the smell was very familiar to Mr. Bush; only he could not call to mind at the moment of what common substance the smell reminded him. "Here," he said, "lend me a knife." So they brought a knife, and Mr. Bush cut the child's head right in half. The knife went through it easily enough, and when the two halves fell apart the child's head turned out to be—what do you think?—why, *soap*! Nothing but a great lump of common yellow soap. The coroner stared at the villagers, and was thankful he had not officially sworn in the jury. The village sensation "caved in," as the Yankees say, *but* the poor woman's character was saved. A striking example of how easily a person's good name may be injured.

—————————

†† Oxfordshire for "something."

Now for the history. It appears that the "child's head, or summut," had been found in a little flue, above a fireplace, in a cottage once occupied by an old woman. This old woman had been in the habit of keeping her bars of yellow soap on a ledge up the chimney; and one day she, by accident, had pushed a bar of soap down the flue. It had in time become melted, and had, by some strange coincidence, assumed the form of a child's head, and thus caused all the fuss that was made about it.

*—also available from—*

# THE COLLINS LIBRARY

# ENGLISH AS SHE IS SPOKE
## BY JOSÉ DA FONSECA AND PEDRO CAROLINO

Perhaps the worst foreign phrasebook ever written, this linguistic train wreck was first published in 1855 and became a classic of unintentional humor. Mark Twain proclaimed that "Nobody can add to the absurdity of this book, nobody can imitate it successfully, nobody can hope to produce its fellow; it is perfect."

"This book has made me laugh so hard it almost hurts… Should be experienced by anyone who loves our language." —*Washington Post*

# THE RIDDLE OF THE TRAVELING SKULL
## BY HARRY STEPHEN KEELER

In dozens of dumbfounding novels, Harry Stephen Keeler ecstatically catapulted the mystery genre into an absurdity that has yet to be equaled. This one begins with a cutting-edge handbag and grows to engulf experimental brain surgery, Legga the Human Spider, and the unlikely asylum state of San Do Mar. Things get stranger from there.

"You cannot possibly dream of anything half so bizarre as the yarn that Mr. Keeler has strung together." —*New York Times*

# LADY INTO FOX
## BY DAVID GARNETT

David Garnett's haunting 1922 debut offers the story of a man, a woman, a fox, and a love that could not be tamed.

"It is the most successful thing of the kind I have ever seen… flawless in style and exposition, altogether an accomplished piece of work." —Joseph Conrad

# TO RUHLEBEN—AND BACK
## BY GEOFFREY PYKE

In 1914, Geoffrey Pyke made his way across wartime Europe on a false passport, a pretty good German accent, and sheer chutzpah. He was eventually captured and ended up in Ruhleben, a horsetrack turned prison. After an escape in broad daylight and a nerve-racking journey across Germany, Pyke wrote the first eyewitness account of a German internment camp. In print for the first time since 1916, his extraordinary book is a college student's sharp-tongued travelogue, an odyssey of hairsbreadth escapes, a sober meditation on imprisonment, and, as Pyke intended, a ripping yarn.

"The war will produce few books of more absorbing interest than this one." —*New York Times*

# THE LUNATIC AT LARGE
## BY J. STORER CLOUSTON

The best-bred lunatics in England live in Clankwood, and Francis Beveridge is that institution's newest resident. Rather than attending the asylum's Saturday dances, though, Beveridge—if that's his real name—goes on the lam in London. And thus, when a traveling German noble finds himself at the luxurious Hotel Mayonaise without a guide to the kingdom's customs, who better to escort him than the amnesiac Englishman who materializes by his side? Beveridge provides the German with much useful knowledge: how to bring rail stations to a standstill, how to fake a rabies attack, and the best way to crash the city's most exclusive clubs—quite literally. A much-loved Victorian comic masterpiece, this is the original anarchic novel that ushered in the age of Wodehouse and Waugh.

—FIND THEM ALL AT STORE.MCSWEENEYS.NET—